BASIC WINEMAKING
BY
BRIAN LEVERETT,
M.PHIL., PH.D.

BASIC WINEMAKING

by

BRIAN LEVERETT,

M.PHIL., PH.D.

Member of the National Guild of Wine and Beer Judges, Co-founder and Editor of *Practical Winemaking and Brewing*. Author of *Winemaking Month by Month*, *Home Beermaking*, etc.

 The Gavin Press

Published by The Gavin Press Limited, 36, Fore Street, Evershot, Dorchester, Dorset.

ISBN 0 905868 10 2

Typeset by Photosetting & Secretarial Services Limited, Yeovil.

Printed by Page Bros (Norwich) Ltd

CONTENTS

Note
It is illegal to sell home-made wines, privately or at sales, exhibitions or other events.

Foreword

The hedgerows of Britain are a natural vineyard, whose bounteous crops of blackberries and elderberries, with often little more addition than some sugar, are waiting to be converted into the traditional wines of the countryside. Winemaking began as a part of the country economy, and like most rural pursuits it was performed with the simplicity that comes with years of experience and knowledge. Then suddenly winemaking moved into the cities, and soon a relatively easy process rapidly became complicated. It required shelves full of chemicals and expensive equipment, all of which if incorrectly used produced inferior rather than better wines. Winemaking became more difficult as its popularity increased.

It would be wrong to suggest that none of the innovations were beneficial, many were, but the problem has been sorting out which items actually make the task easier and which are just a further complication. Moreover winemaking today is not simply an autumn operation. Now, thanks to a better knowledge of what goes into producing a wine, we have been able to formulate recipes from ingredients that our ancestors never considered as a source of a beverage. The innovation that has changed the whole nature of winemaking is the availability of grape and other fruit concentrates, making us independent of the season and allowing the winemaker, with the minimum of effort, equipment and experience, to rival the drinks made by the professional.

This book is written for the person who wishes to make his wine in an uncomplicated way, to be able to produce drinks, if he so desires, at any time of the year, from any of the available materials, and at the same time obtain the very best drinks it is possible to make.

One of the most common causes of failure in any field is a lack of understanding of the basic principles involved. In the initial chapters I have attempted to explain the theories behind all the winemaking operations, and discussed the reasoning that went into the compounding of the recipes, all of which I have made and enjoyed drinking.

I hope that you obtain as much pleasure from country winemaking as I have over more years than I care to remember.

BRIAN LEVERETT

May, 1982

Chapter One

Why Make your own Wines?

Economy has always been put forward as the main reason for making wines at home, but this is only part of the reason for the increasing popularity of home winemaking. Whilst many activities that were based on saving money, such as raising chickens in the back garden, have almost died out, winemaking grows from strength to strength. Today virtually everyone has a demijohn of wine bubbling away in the kitchen, including many who could afford to buy all the wine that they require, and although we must look to other reasons for the universal popularity of the hobby, the economic side can not be ignored. At today's prices it is possible to enjoy a bottle of wine a day for less than a pound a week, which is only a twelfth to a fifteenth of the price of commercial wines.

The recent rapid increase in popularity of winemaking has gone hand in hand with the improvement in quality that has occurred as our knowledge of winemaking has increased. Today we produce wines to satisfy the most discerning palates. No longer does homemade wine mean a sweet liquid, often tinged with vinegar, that has more in common with sweet and sour sauce than a beverage. There is no need now to apologise to a guest for offering him a glass of homemade wine any more than you think of making excuses for serving a slice of homemade cake or a lunch you have cooked yourself. Country wines are accepted as part of our way of life.

Add the sense of achievement of converting a few berries into a gallon of wine to the economy and quality of the drink produced, and it is at once apparent why home winemaking is now one of the most popular hobbies.

Winemaking is a simple operation, but the beginner is often confused as to where to start due to the wide range of methods and ingredients that are now available to make drinks. Which method is most suitable will depend on your own personal requirements. Kits and concentrates produce wines with less effort in a far shorter period of time, but tend to cost more. Fruits are cheaper, tend to give more satisfaction, but require more effort and patience. Both result in good quality wines. Many winemakers use both, and once it is realised that you make wine you will almost certainly be given kits at Christmas and birthdays, so you will be able to decide for yourself the relative merits of each method.

As well as the new ingredients, and many of the most useful are not sold specifically for winemaking, a large amount of equipment has appeared on the market. Much of the equipment has contributed to the increase in quality and the ease with which wines can be made. Unfortunately this proliferation has served to confuse the new-comer. Until you are aware that you intend to continue winemaking it is advisable to purchase only the minimum of equipment. Some winemakers never add to the basic items and yet continually make excellent wines.

ESSENTIAL EQUIPMENT

White Plastic Bucket Wines contain acids and these acids are capable of dissolving poisons out of equipment, so it is important that only white plastic buckets or food buckets are used for the initial fermentation. It is advisable to buy a purpose-made fermentation bucket, and these come complete with a tight-fitting lid to stop the entry of germs. The old idea of covering the bucket with a cloth, tray, or piece of wood contributed much to the vinegars that used to be produced. Since you need only start one gallon of wine at a time one bucket will suffice, although you may wish to acquire others at a later date.

Demijohns These are the gallon jars (although most hold slightly more than this quantity) in which the wine is fermented. You will require one for every single gallon of wine that you are currently making. Brown demijohns tend to be far cheaper than clear glass. They are just as satisfactory, although it is more difficult to see if the wine is clearing. They even possess one advantage over clear glass in that the brown glass cuts down on the transmission of light which tends to destroy the colour in red wines. The suggested method of economising is to use plastic containers. Many of these could affect the taste of the wine and should be avoided, except in the case of sherry fives which can be used for making five gallon batches of wines.

Airlock The airlock is perhaps the most essential piece of the winemaker's equipment as it allows the carbon dioxide to escape, and yet stops the entry of air which not only attacks the wine chemically, but also carries air-borne bacteria and yeast which will destroy the wine. You may buy any design of airlock as they all work efficiently.

Racking Tube Racking is the separation of the liquid from solid material formed during fermentation. Separating the liquid is essential if a quality wine is to be made, and this is achieved by syphoning the liquid from one demijohn to another with a racking tube. Again there are several different designs on the market, and although all can be used to perform the operation successfully, it is best to choose the easiest to clean as they can be a source of infection.

Sieving Bag In order to separate the solid material from the liquid at the initial fermentation stage, it is advisable to make a sieving bag. Since this must retain the solid, but allow the liquid to filter through, use a piece of strong nylon material with threads not too closely interwoven. You will require a piece three feet by two feet and sewn in a V shape. The top should now fit over the rim of a bucket. To avoid the danger of slipping tie the bag under the rim of the bucket. One method of overcoming the problem is to sew tying tapes to the bag itself.

Corking Machine The appearance of a wine is important. Few things are more satisfying than the 'plop' that is heard as the cork is withdrawn from a well-presented bottle. This level of presentation will only be achieved if you invest in a corking machine and some attractive labels. Whilst this adds slightly to the cost, it is unwise to spoil the ship for a ha'p'orth of tar.

Hydrometer So entrenched in the use of the hydrometer have winemakers become that few even realise that it is possible to make good wines without recourse to it. The hydrometer measures the gravity of the wine and hence the quantity of sugar that is present. This allows you to follow the course of fermentation and to estimate the percentage of alcohol present. An essential piece of equipment for those who wish to develop their own recipes and delve into the theory of winemaking. Both techniques are beyond the scope of this book and for information on how to use the hydrometer and its role in recipe formulation you are advised to consult *Winemaking Month By Month*.

Acid Testing Kits These again are only necessary if you intend producing your own recipes. As the name implies they measure the amount of acid in the liquid. Where you are following the recipes provided in this book you may ignore the acid levels, for although these will depend to some extent on the season, the variety of fruit and the time at which the harvest was gathered, the variation is very small compared with the total and will not be detectable in the finished wine.

Filter With the demand for wines that are ready for drinking in far shorter periods, and a degree of clarity comparable with commercial wines, a variety of filters have become available. A wine correctly made to a good recipe will, in time – often a quite short period – clear without any further help and a filter is by no means essential. They tend to be an extra, expensive complication best avoided by the novice.

Chemicals One of the biggest advantages that the modern winemaker has over his predecessors is the ready availability of a range of synthetic chemicals that make the task easier and help to remove any danger of making unsatisfactory wines. Do not allow the idea of adding artificial chemicals to deter you, providing you buy from a home-brew shop or a pharmacy you can rest assured that they have all been thoroughly tested for purity and that they will have no ill effect on either you or your wines. Should you still wish to avoid using them you may, but it does increase the possibility of cloudy, unstable wines.

Sterilising Agents Special compounds for sterilising equipment can be bought. You may either use these, Milton or household bleach. If you use household bleach then you must ensure that the equipment is thoroughly washed after use (see instructions on sterilisation). Although it is just as important to sterilise the fruit UNDER NO CIRCUMSTANCES USE CHEMICALS SOLD TO STERILISE EQUIPMENT OR BLEACH ON FRUIT. Apart from any dangers of poisoning they will react with the fruit and afford an undrinkable wine.

Campden Tablets and Sodium Metabisulphite Sodium metabisulphite, sometimes referred to simply as bisulphite, releases sulphur dioxide on reaction with acid. The sulphur dioxide will help to stop a wine from refermenting, but it is not completely effective. It will not stop a vigorously fermenting wine, nor will it always prohibit a wine from refermenting if it has residual sugar present and the temperature suddenly rises. The most important use of this chemical in winemaking is to stop the wine reacting with the air. This reaction not only changes the colour of the wine, it can lead to unacceptable tastes. Such tastes are particularly noticeable with very light, dry wines. With the heavier wines not only does a slight oxidation not detract from the flavour of the wine, it often enhances it. Consequently the use of sodium metabisulphite is not essential with all wines. Where it is needed instruction is given in the individual recipe. Because of the ability that sulphur dioxide has to kill germs, it is often recommended as a sterilising agent for both equipment and fruit. Unfortunately it is not as effective for equipment as the stronger chemicals sold for this purpose and its use is not suitable, except in special cases, with fruit. The boiling water method is far more effective. Sodium metabisulphite is the main constituent of Campden tablets. These are far easier to use and measure than the pure chemical, and their use is preferred wherever sulphur dioxide is required.

Enzymes Fruit contains the non-fermentable carbohydrate pectin. Some fruits and most vegetables contain starch. The concentration of both these compounds in the liquid is enhanced by the use of boiling water, and if either of these are allowed to remain there is a danger that the wine will never completely clear. In order to avoid this problem it is usual to add either one, or both of the wine clearing enzymes depending on the ingredients that are being used to make the wine. Enzymes are substances that are made in either plants or animals and perform specific chemical reactions. They are extremely delicate chemicals whose structures are destroyed by large excesses of alcohol or high temperatures. To obtain the maximum benefit from enzymes they should be added together with the yeast. The two enzymes that are used in winemaking are PECTIC ENZYME which destroys pectin, and AMYLASE which converts any starch into the fermentable sugar MALTOSE. The quantity to add to the liquid is given on the container.

Yeast Nutrients Yeast derives most of its food from sugar, but it also requires other nutrients. With many ingredients such as grapes there are usually sufficient minerals in the liquid and no further additions are necessary. But some winemaking fruits, which unlike grapes that provide the wine with everything that it requires, are only used to give flavour. When using these materials it is important to add the extra minerals and vitamins separately. This is most conveniently achieved by adding yeast nutrient, which consists mainly of salts of ammonia and phosphate together with vitamin B_1 (thiamin), although most of the proprietory yeast foods contain additional compounds. It will do no harm to add nutrient even if there is sufficient naturally present in the fruit. Do not, however, exceed the recommended amount as a large excess can result in the drink possessing a salty taste. Many yeast are sold together with nutrient. This can be seen as white crystals between the brown pieces of yeast. When using this type of yeast there is no need to add additional nutrient.

Citric Acid Yeast requires the correct acid level to ferment successfully. Failure to provide enough acid can result in the wine either ceasing to work or possessing a medicinal taste. Some fruits have enough natural acid, some even have too much, and only a limited amount may be used to avoid making a wine with a far too acidic taste. Where flowers, roots and grains are used it is necessary to add extra acid. The traditional way of doing this was to add the juice of a lemon. The disadvantage of this was the cost of the lemon, the varying amounts of juice that could be obtained from individual fruits, and the danger of allowing pieces of the pith, which gives the wine a bitter taste, entering the liquid. The active ingredient responsible for much of the taste and flavour of the lemon is citric acid. By buying and using pure citric acid it is possible to control accurately the amount of acid that is added to any wine.

With the search to make wines more similar in taste to those that you can buy, winemakers have experimented with MALIC ACID – found naturally in apples, TARTARIC ACID – obtained from grapes and the acid of milk – LACTIC. These and various combinations it is claimed result in better wines. Such improvements are very slight and are really only applicable to those people attempting to produce show wines.

Unless you intend making special wines for exhibition it is advisable to begin with only the minimum of equipment and to restrict the number of chemicals that you employ to a similar small number. MUCH OF THE POPULARITY OF WINEMAKING LIES IN ITS SIMPLICITY. FOR THE BEST RESULTS IT IS BETTER TO ADOPT A COMPLETELY UNCOMPLICATED APPROACH.

Chapter Two

What is Wine?

Wine is defined as the juice of the grape fermented in its region of origin. Our wine obviously does not fit this description, and when we use the term we are referring to country wines. Country wines are drinks that rely on added sugar to provide most, or all, of the alcohol.

Only the liquid from grapes provides all of the constituents that are involved in making a wine. Alcohol derived solely from sugar is a tasteless, thin, bland drink that is completely unappetising. In order to overcome this problem it is necessary to blend a variety of fruits which will provide the wine with flavour, astringency – acid and tannin – and body. This can be achieved by using several different combinations of vegetable materials. At first sight it might appear that any formulation of fruits will produce a wine and up to some extent this is true, but a worthwhile drink will only be achieved if all of the factors that constitute a wine are in balance. The main constituents of a wine are discussed below.

Flavour Virtually all ingredients contribute to the overall flavour of the wine, although the finished wine may not always possess a flavour that is readily identifiable with the ingredients used. Young wines often retain the true characteristics of the starting material, but as the wine ages the taste gradually changes until usually it is not possible to ascertain what the drink was prepared from. This occurs as a result of the interaction between the alcohol formed, the acids present, together with other materials produced during fermentation affording a totally new taste. If, therefore, you wish to enjoy fruity wines then you should always drink them whilst they are still young, that is when they are between three and nine months old.

Body This is the general name given to the dissolved solids and liquids other than alcohol in the wine. Drinks that are low in these materials taste thin and are only suitable for drinking with a meal. Wines with a reasonable degree of body are far less harsh, and slight off flavours such as those produced by oxidation are less noticeable. Body is given to a wine by raisins, sultanas, grape juice conentrate, bananas, a high concentrate of fruit and certain vegetables such as pea pods and runner beans.

Acidity Much of the acid required for winemaking will be contained in the flavour providing fruit, and the quantity of the acid rather than the flavour is in some cases the limiting factor in deciding the amount of a particular type of fruit that may be used. Extra acid may be provided by blending a second type of fruit into the must, adding oranges or lemons, using a carton of orange or grapefuit juice or adding a can of a high acid fruit such as gooseberries. The cheapest way of providing additional acid is to add citric acid, as previously discussed.

Tannin Tannin is a complex chemical, somewhat similar to an acid, which gives the wine a characteristic zest. Wines lacking in tannin tend to be flat and insipid. It is thought that tannin helps to clarify a wine. Tannin is found naturally in many fruits especially in association with the seeds and skin. Additional tannin may be provided by incorporating raisins or sultanas in the recipe, or adding a cup of cold tea to a gallon of the liquid. Grape tannin can be bought as a powder or in solution, either form is a useful way of providing the extra tannin.

Sugar Although we often add three pounds or more of sugar to a gallon of wine it presents the least problem of all the ingredients. Generally granulated – household – sugar is the most suitable. There are more expensive forms of sugar but the yeast is unable to appreciate any difference, and the final result will taste the same irrespective of the type of sugar used. There is one exception and that is demerara sugar, which imparts a slightly burnt flavour to the wine, similar to that found in a Madeira. Such a taste blends well with a heavy sweet dessert wine and will help to give it an aged effect whilst it is still young.

Having compounded the recipe and added the necessary water the winemaker has little control over the actual wine-making process. This is performed entirely by the yeast. This does not mean that you can be careless with your winemaking, you must provide the right conditions for the yeast and ensure that the environment is not such as to destroy the wine produced. Providing that you supply the yeast with its few simple requirements it will do the rest for you.

Yeast is a fungus, and it obtains its energy from sugar, converting it into alcohol in the process. At the same time the yeast brings about other changes in the liquid and the alcohol formed itself changes some of the other chemicals present, resulting in the finished liquid bearing very little resemblance to what it was like prior to fermentation.

Initial Fermentation Yeast, although it is only a simple plant has a rather complex life history. When it comes into contact with a food source it begins to multiply rapidly. This stage in its life can be seen as a frothy head on the top of the liquid. During this time the yeast requires a large quantity of air, and throughout the first stage, termed the initial fermentation, it is important that there is an air space at least equal to that occupied by the liquid. The length of time that the froth will remain will depend upon many factors, including the quantity of sugar present and the temperature, but it usually lasts from four to twelve days. The end of this initial stage occurs when the frothy head ceases, to be replaced with the gentle escape of bubbles.

Secondary Fermentation The yeast then enters the secondary fermentation stage. During this period far less reproduction occurs, and only sufficient new cells to replace those that die are formed. Due to the drop in the breeding rate, air is no longer required by the yeast and care should be taken to ensure that the oxygen once essential to the yeast life cycle is excluded completely from the wine. An excess of air for any period of time between now and the drinking stage will result in either a chemical or bacterial attack.

At the commencement of the secondary fermentation the liquid is still cloudy, due to suspended matter. Gradually, as the fermentation continues, the wine begins to clear and a heavy sediment develops at the bottom of the demijohn. This sediment consists of dead yeast cells together with vegetable material that separates from the solution. The sediment will gradually begin to decompose giving the wine a musty taste, so it is important that the liquid is separated from the solid. This separation should be conducted as soon as the sediment is a quarter of an inch thick.

The Effect of Alcohol As fermentation continues the level of alcohol begins to build up. Although the yeast produces alcohol, this alcohol will kill the yeast as soon as it reaches a concentration of 16-18%. The yeast's tolerance to its own alcohol is the limiting factor to the strength of wine that it is possible to obtain. Long before the yeast is killed its activity begins to slow down, as is seen by a gradual decrease in the rate at which the gas carbon dioxide escapes from the airlock.

To make wines of the maximum alcohol level requires special care. It is not advisable to add more than three pounds of sugar to a gallon of the liquid, giving a wine of about 14% alcohol. If larger amounts of sugar are added the yeast is often killed by dehydration. To overcome this danger add only three pounds at the beginning and feed the extra sugar as a syrup after each racking. In this manner it is possible to steadily build up the alcohol level to a maximum. Due to this danger of dehydration it is essential that at least the vast majority of the sugar is dissolved at the time that the liquid is prepared for fermentation.

The conversion of sugar into alcohol is only part of the winemaking process. As the percentage of alcohol increases then other changes occur in the liquid itself. The first task in winemaking is to compound a liquid – termed the must – which contains the necessary body and flavouring materials. The initial operations in winemaking are all directed towards this end, and on how successful you are in dissolving out the maximum material will depend the quality of the wine. Wine is made from a liquid, not a solid, and every attempt must be made to liquify the solids or divide them fully in order that water will dissolve out the maximum amount of the soluble materials present.

The boiling water – far more efficient than cold water – will dissolve out certain classes of compounds whilst the newly formed alcohol will leach out substances that are insoluble in water. During the early stages of fermentation when alcohol is being formed in the presence of the solid fruit and vegetables, important materials are being added to the must. After the initial fermentation period all the useful ingredients in the solid will have entered the liquid, and the solid will begin to decompose. In order to stop these decomposition products from spoiling the wine it is necessary to strain.

Maturation As the first alcohol is formed it enters into a complex series of reactions, the termination of which results in a bottle of wine. How long this process takes will depend upon the exact nature of the wine and the amount of alcohol present. Light, low-alcohol wines require the shortest maturation periods whilst the sweet, heavy, high-alcohol dessert wines need the longest period.

There is a common misconception that the quality of any wine is directly related to the age. This is undoubtedly true of certain vintages of the world's greatest commercial wines. Certain clarets and vintage ports undoubtedly improve with time. This is due in part to the loss of excess tannin, but even in the commercial field some wines reach their zenith after six months or a year. Once a wine has peaked it then begins, often quite fast, to deteriorate. With country wines there is seldom an advantage of storing for prolonged periods. The best approach is try one bottle, and if it is ready drink and enjoy the rest. If it is not then wait and sample another bottle later.

Styles of Wine Originally country wines were made for one purpose only, drinking in the evenings with friends. Whilst that is still the most popular use, many people now try to imitate the commercial styles of wine, and we can now make a full range of drinks. The type of wine that is required greatly affects the ingredients that are used to make the wine.

By adjusting the recipe some ingredients, such as elder-berries, can be used to make every known style of wines. Others, such as dates and figs, produce a particular flavour that is only suitable for dessert wines. Flowers, which only yield the delicate bouquet in a wine, are really suitable just for table wines, although some vintners incorporate them in their dessert wines.

It remains very much a personal choice whether you make your wines for a specific purpose or to simply enjoy as you relax. When making wines for a purpose the following is a useful general guide.

APERITIFS	Apple, herb flavoured and tomato wines, imitation sherries as made from prunes or parsnip.
TABLE WINES	
Red Dry	Blackberry, elderberry, concentrate and kit wines.
White Dry	Apple wine, citrus fruit wines, fruit juice wines concentrate and kit wines.
White Sweet	Any of the above artificially sweetened.
SOCIAL WINES	For drinking with friends. Virtually any fruit wines, wines made from less common ingredients are useful as conversation openers.

DESSERT WINES Sweet elderberry or blackberry, peach and any containing a pound of raisins or sultanas per gallon.

WHEN WE UNDERSTAND THE NATURE OF WINE WE ARE FAR MORE LIKELY TO TAKE THAT LITTLE EXTRA CARE TO ENSURE WE HAVE A REALLY GOOD BEVERAGE.

Chapter Three

How is Wine Made?

Whilst different ingredients require slightly different approaches, there are general operations that one applies to all wines. Such variations as are necessary are discussed in the individual recipes.

Sterilisation At any stage in the winemaking process the drink can be irreversibly destroyed by either spoilage yeast or bacteria, and it is essential to ensure that all of the equipment is maintained in a sterile state. This can be achieved in one of three ways. You can either buy a wine equipment sterilising agent and use it according to the manufacturer's instructions. You may boil or place ALL of the equipment in the oven at 212°F (100°C), however apart from the often impracticability of the method plastics will become pliable or even melt at this temperature. The most convenient method is to use ordinary household bleach. A word of caution is necessary when using this liquid. Bleach is a poison, and it will also damage the lungs if it is inhaled. To avoid any danger place all of the winemaking equipment in the fermenting bucket, then pour about an egg-cup full of the bleach, (do not attempt to measure it) in the container. Add about a quart of water and place the lid on the bucket. Leave for half an hour. Pour the liquid down the sink and fill the bucket with tap water. Take out each item and either hold under the tap, or wash with constant swirling. All equipment treated in this way will be completely safe and free from germs. IT IS IMPORTANT THAT ALL EQUIPMENT IS STERILISED IMMEDIATELY PRIOR TO USE AT ALL STAGES IN THE WINEMAKING OPERATION.

Preparing the Must The more thorough the manner in which the fruit is broken up the better will be the quality of the wine obtained. Ideally a press should be used, but as few people will wish to go to this trouble or expense, a large liquidiser is an adequate substitute, though again only a minority of wine-makers possess one. The recipes given have all been developed on the basis of chopping or mincing the fruit and covering with boiling water. The water must be boiling to kill the wild yeast and bacteria present on the skins of the fruit. Should you allow these to remain they will dominate and take over from the added yeast, giving off flavours, or even turning the wine into vinegar. There are some traditional recipes that do not even advocate the addition of yeast relying entirely on the natural yeasts. Whilst this works on some occasions it is a hit and miss affair. Homemade wines are cheap but if your efforts have to be thrown down the sink it is a very expensive wastage.

When making a gallon of wine it is advisable to add a quarter to half the volume as boiling water. As soon as the mixture is cool enough to handle, the sugar to be added at this stage should be poured in and stirred until dissolved. This involves far less work than making up a separate sugar syrup solution. Once the sugar has dissolved a further two pints of cold tap water should be added. Never make the volume up to eight pints at this stage as some liquid may be extracted from the fruit and if the total exceeds the volume of the demijohn the residual must is wasted.

Whilst the must is cooling it is open to infection so cover the bucket; any air-borne germs that enter will be insignificant compared with the yeast that is provided. The yeast must not be added until the liquid has dropped to at least 75°F (23.5°C).

Adding the Yeast The only yeast that should be used for winemaking is a GENERAL WINEMAKING YEAST. This is dried yeast that is prepared by dehydrating an active yeast. The outside of the granules consist of dead cells, and these form a layer that will protect the yeast inside for several months. When the dried yeast is added to a sugar solution at the correct temperature, the live cells regain their activity and fermentation commences. Such yeast will not keep indefinitely, and as you can not tell how long it has been on the shelf, if you only intend to make a small quantity of wine buy individual sachets. When regularly making large quantities purchase a drum and add one level teaspoonful to each gallon batch that you brew.

The most important aspect of fermentation is the maintenance of the correct temperature 65-70°F (18.5-21°C). Failure to do this will result in prolonged fermentation or even a stuck fermentation – when the wine prematurely ceases working – resulting in cordial production. Most houses possess a suitable area where the temperature is at the desired level. During the summer several successful ferments are conducted on window sills, and throughout the winter adjacent to a central-heating radiator. Wines are still successfully made in airing cupboards. This approach whilst being the most universally practised is not always satisfactory if you wish to produce large quantities of wines. Your homebrew shop will stock a variety of heating mantles, belts and other devices which will maintain a steady heat. Alternatively you may build a fermenting cabinet, which consists of a wooden box large enough to hold all the demijohns that you require to be held at a controlled temperature. A hole is bored into the side of the box and electrical flex is passed through. Connect the flex to the thermostat and then connect up to either a small element heater or a 60 watt light bulb. A fermenting cabinet is an extremely useful piece of equipment that any home handyman can make with the minimum of effort.

THE LIQUID SHOULD BE KEPT AT 65-70°F (18.5-21°C) FROM THE TIME

THAT THE YEAST IS ADDED TO THE WINE UNTIL THE FINAL BUBBLE HAS ESCAPED FROM THE AIRLOCK. FAILURE TO MAINTAIN AN ADEQUATE TEMPERATURE IS ONE OF THE MOST COMMON CAUSES OF STUCK FERMENTS. At the same time that the yeast is added to the liquid, any recommended enzymes should also be provided.

The Start of Fermentation The first activity in the wine should be observed within 12-24 hours of adding the yeast, when a few bubbles will be seen escaping from the surface. It is often easier to hear the bubbles escaping than actually seeing them in the early stages. Should you fail to detect any sign of activity within 48 hours immediately buy a new sample of yeast – the original may have been defective – and add this to the must. Failure to do this will result in the wine becoming vinegar. Failures of this type are very rare unless the yeast has been stored for several months.

Remove the cover of the fermenting bucket each day and stir the liquid thoroughly. This often omitted stage performs several useful functions. It helps to dissolve extra air at the same time dispersing much of the carbon dioxide above the liquid; it helps the break-up of the fruit and the extraction of flavours, and stops the settling out of the denser sugar solution at the bottom of the container. Whilst the initial fermentation is proceeding the large volume of carbon dioxide that is generated will protect the liquid from bacteria attack, and so the lid may be removed frequently without fear of infection. The carbon dioxide will protect the wine for a short period (usually about a week) after the initial head has subsided, but do not delay unduly the straining of the liquid and the transference to the demijohn.

Straining As soon as you are sure that the head has subsided, place the straining bag (sterilised by boiling in water) over the top of a second plastic bucket and pour the liquid and solid into the new bucket. Allow the bag to drain but do not squeeze. Immediately transfer the liquid into the demijohn. You will find that the liquid probably reaches the shoulder of the vessel, although there may be tremendous variations in the actual volume depending upon the quantity of liquid that is obtained from the fruit. Fit the airlock and return to the fermenting temperature and leave for one week. At the end of the week the demijohn should be topped-up to within an inch below the rubber bung. By delaying the topping-up in this way, should the initial fermentation have been incomplete there is no danger of the wine frothing over the top and into the airlock.

Racking Almost as soon as the wine is placed in the demijohn a layer of dead yeast cells – termed lees – will be seen to form at the bottom of the container. After about a month to six weeks this will be about $\frac{1}{4}$ inch (0.5 cms) in depth and at this stage the wine should be racked. If you are in doubt as to when to rack the wine the first racking can·be postponed until the wine has been fermenting for three months, further delay will lead to a musty taste in the finished wine.

Racking is simply the syphoning off of the liquid from the solid. This is best achieved by placing the demijohn containing the wine on the top of the kitchen work surface and placing a second clean demijohn on the floor. Place the racking tube in the higher demijohn. Most racking tubes have a bend or similar device at the bottom to ensure that the tube itself does not enter the lees and bring this across with the liquid. Should your tube not possess such a device then hold the base of the tube about an inch (2.5 cms) from the top of the lees. Now suck through the tube. When the liquid arrives at the end of the tube place a finger or thumb over it and transfer into the lower container. Allow all of the liquid to syphon across.

Due to the volume occupied by the lees and the inevitable loss through transference there will be an airspace of between an inch and two inches at the top of the demijohn. Fill this space with tap water, or, if the recipe demands, sugar syrup. The slight dilution effect of up to two rackings will have been allowed for in the recipe, and thus extra water rather than weakening the wine actually improves the overall quality. Usually one racking is insufficient to remove all of the heavy sediment that forms, although with some of the quicker wines they can be drunk after the first racking. If the wine has not finished fermenting by the time of the first racking, return to the recommended temperature and allow the process to continue. When fermentation ceases, if the only cloudiness is due to suspended yeast cells it usually falls clear almost immediately, and at this stage it can be given its final racking as described above. However on occasions it is slower in clarifying, in which case the second racking should be delayed until three months after the first, but no longer. Rack and make up to the level again with tap water. Only very occasionally is a third racking necessary. Should this occur then the wine is again racked after a three month period, and this then should be topped up with either a similar finished wine or a solution of 3 oz (90 gms) of sugar in $\frac{1}{2}$ pint ($\frac{1}{4}$ litre) of tap water. NEVER ADD A SUGAR SYRUP TO A CLEAR WINE AS REFERMENTATION WILL RESULT AND THE WINE WILL AGAIN FORM A YEAST SEDIMENT.

It is at the final fermentation stage that a Campden tablet, if recommended, should be added. Always thoroughly crush the tablet between two teaspoons, as failure to do this will result in the chemical dissolving only very slowly, making it ineffective, and the objectionable taste that it imparts to a wine lingering on for several weeks. Where wines have been treated with Campden tablets they do initially possess a strong chemical taste. If only one tablet is used this seldom lasts more than a fortnight, whilst with two tablets, which are more effective in offering protection, the taste and odour can linger for several weeks.

Storage and Drinking When the final racking has been performed and the wine is clear, it may be drunk almost immediately or stored. Storing for a few months allows the wine to mellow and it loses much of its harsh taste. Large-scale maturation, in which the wine is stored in the demijohn, not only appears to produce the best results it is also the most convenient way of storing. When storing in a demijohn, because refermentation is always a possibility, fit an airlock and ensure that it is kept primed with water. Demijohns are expensive items and in the early stages of winemaking you may well not have enough to allow you to store in this way, so simply bottle. Sooner or later you will have to bottle the wine AS UNDER NO CIRCUMSTANCES SHOULD YOU POUR GLASSES STRAIGHT FROM THE DEMIJOHN, THE AIR SPACE ABOVE A FINISHED WINE WILL CAUSE IT TO DECOMPOSE VERY RAPIDLY.

Always store bottles of wine on their side in order that the cork remains moist and does not shrink allowing air to enter. The temperature at which country wines are stored is probably not as important as it is with commercial wines, but try to avoid extremes of temperature. The garage is not a good place for wines as they can become hazy as a result of the sudden drop in temperatures during the frost season.

Chapter Four

What Can Go Wrong?

Providing you take the few simple precautions discussed in the previous chapter winemaking is easy and you are unlikely to experience many problems. However, because there are so many factors beyond our control such as the quality of fruit, difference in ingredients – for example sultanas originating from a variety of countries – and the fact that the recipes have been developed by one person using his particular fruit source, very occasionally something does go wrong and disappointment results. Except for problems caused by lack of hygiene it is generally possible to cure the faults.

Listed below are some of the most common problems, together with their causes, and where possible the remedy.

Stuck Ferment This occurs when the yeast is either killed or loses its activity because the conditions are unsuitable for its growth. The most common cause of stuck ferment is too low a temperature, and simply placing the wine in a warmer environment often overcomes the problem. Should this fail then you require a new sample of yeast. In order that the fresh yeast can function correctly it will need to go through an initial fermentation stage in the presence of excess air. Divide the wine into two, placing each half in a separate demijohn. Add a teaspoonful of yeast, place in a warm atmosphere and shake the half filled demijohn daily. Allow the vigorous fermentation to build up and then die down again before recombining the two halves in one demijohn. Should the wine not commence refermenting after this treatment then the problem is almost certainly due to too large a quantity of sugar present. To overcome this problem add a half a pint ($\frac{1}{4}$ litre) of water to each of the halves in the separate demijohn. Again add yeast and check the temperature. After this treatment the wine will start to referment. When you recombine the two batches of liquid you will have a pint of liquid in excess. This unfortunately has to be destroyed as odd pints, left to ferment in milk bottles with cotton wool in the top, almost invariably turn to an undrinkable brew. The air that is allowed into the wine during the restart of fermentation is unlikely to cause problems as initially the liquid is not suitable for biological activity, otherwise the yeast would survive. As the yeast begins working the carbon dioxide will again protect the liquid. This high carbon dioxide level will also protect the wine from chemical attack.

Difficulty To Clear Clarification is one of the most complex aspects of winemaking, depending on several items, including minute traces of minerals in tap water. Often wines clarify simply on standing, but if the wine is not clear a year after fermentation has ceased it will probably never be brilliant. There is no single method applicable to all clearance problems. Your first method of approach to the problem should be to add a proprietary wine finings to the liquid. Alternatively you can use the white of an egg. Shake the white of an egg in a pint of the wine. The suspension, which is sufficient to clear up to five gallons of wine, should be added to the wine and shaken for about ten minutes. The mixture must then be allowed to stand for forty-eight hours. Next rack or decant the cleared wine from the sediment. Either of these treatments are extremely effective when fairly large particles in suspension are responsible for the cloudiness. Where microscopic particles cause the haze it will still persist after this treatment and it is unlikely that you will be able to remove it completely. Usually these persistent hazes are due to either pectin or starch, and only form if insufficient or no enzymes were employed initially. Decide from the nature of the starting materials whether the cause is most likely to be due to starch – this will apply if root vegetables, bananas or cereals were used to make the wine – or pectin, which occurs with most fruits, and can be particularly troublesome if certain types of sultanas or raisins are minced. Add either amylase, pectic enzyme or both. Neither enzyme is as effective if added at the end of the ferment, but often they are capable of reducing the haze to an acceptable level at this stage.

The Wine Has A Cheese-Like Or Other Strange Flavour Very light wines such as those made from flowers will, if not prepared and kept under hygienic conditions, be liable to attack by spoilage yeasts which then cause them to develop cheese-like or similar objectionable tastes. Depending on how early the taste is detected it is possible to save the wine. Add two crushed Campden tablets to a gallon of wine and leave to stand until the taste of the added chemical has disappeared. Taste the wine, and if you find it acceptable then drink the wine quickly, as such a wine will be liable to reinfection. Do not leave any wine with an off flavour as it will rapidly get worse.

White Specks Develop On The Top Of The Wine This is termed flowers of wine and is another type of infection. The flecks break down the alcohol in the wine to carbon dioxide. Treatment is almost always successful if the wine is treated, as soon as the flecks appear, with Campden tablets as described above.

The Wine Has A Vinegar Taste Again this results from infection and is usually, but not always associated with a wine stored under air. It is impossible to treat such a wine and it must be destroyed or else other wines could become infected.

The Wine Starts To Referment This usually occurs from May through the summer months and results from the yeast regaining its activity as a result of the sudden rise in the temperature. This only occurs with sweet wines that contain a small quantity of residual sugar, it is never observed in a completely dry wine. The solution to the problem lies in storing in a cooler room. If you possess sufficient you may return the wine to a demijohn and allow it to complete its fermentation. Providing that the corks are not too tightly placed in the bottles the worst that can happen from refermenting is that they will be blown out of the bottles.

The Wine Is Not Sweet Enough Unless the wine has fermented to an alcohol concentration of 16-18% it will invariably start fermenting again if there is any residual sugar present. This presents a problem for those who enjoy a sweet table wine, of 12% or less alcohol. The easiest way to overcome the problem is to keep a stock sugar syrup solution by you, prepared from dissolving half a pound of sugar (225 gms) in a quarter of a pint (125 ml) of water. Add sugar to the wine, to taste, immediately prior to serving. The small quantity of sugar syrup used will not dilute the flavour, acidity and alcohol appreciably. Do not attempt to add saccharin or artificial sweeteners to a wine as they almost always develop a bitter taste on standing.

The Wine Is Too Acid It is often recommended that chalk is added to decrease the acidity of a wine. It can be difficult to judge the correct quantity to add and often the addition of chalk produces a cloudiness in the wine. Over acidity, or an excess of any flavour that you find spoils a wine can be overcome by blending with a wine that is low in the particular characteristic.

An even simpler solution to the excess acid is to add strong sugar syrup to taste. Sweetness numbs the palate and part of the taste of the acid is undetectable. Next time that you make any wine you have found too acid in the past, reduce any citric acid that you add to the must by a quarter. Where no extra acid is incorporated in the recipe you should decrease the weight of the main ingredient by a similar amount.

The Wine Loses Its Colour Red wines change to a brown colour as part of the ageing process. The colour change is accelerated by light. To slow down the process store your wine in green or brown bottles and never let them stand in direct sunlight. Any oxygen present will have similar adverse effects upon the colour of the wine. White wines acquire a brown tinge as a result of similar poor storage, and future batches should be treated in the same way. Dark colour can be removed by treatment with either caesin or charcoal. As with all chemical treatments the wine after the operation usually loses something as well as that you are seeking to cure and the complication is best avoided.

PREVENTION IS ALWAYS BETTER THAN CURE, AND ALL THE FORE-GOING PROBLEMS CAN BE AVOIDED SIMPLY BY DEVELOPING A GOOD WINEMAKING TECHNIQUE.

Chapter Five

Wines of the Hedgerow

Winemaking probably started in Britain with the fruits of the hedgerow. Not only are these the cheapest of wines requiring only a few ingredients in addition to the sugar, but they are amongst the best wines that can be obtained.

Blackberry Wines Blackberries are relatively high in acid and no addition is necessary where more than 2 lb of fruit are used per gallon. Never allow blackberry wine to ferment for prolonged periods in the presence of the fruit as the pips will give the wine a woody taste.

3½ lb blackberries	1575 gms
½ lb sultanas	225 gms
3 lb sugar	1350 gms
Pectic enzyme	
Yeast	
Water to one gallon	4.5 litres

Place the washed and stalked blackberries in a bucket and thoroughly mash with either a potato masher or a fork. Add the sugar and six pints (3.5 litres) of boiling water. Allow to cool to 65-70°F (18.5-21°C) and add the yeast and pectic enzyme. After three days strain the liquid into a second bucket and provide the sultanas which should be lightly chopped. Ferment the mixture of liquid and solid for a fortnight, then strain again and transfer to a demijohn, top up if necessary and fit an airlock.

Blackberry & Apple Wine

3 lb blackberries	1350 gms
2 lb fallen dessert apples	900 gms
2¾ lb sugar	1250 gms
Pectic enzyme	
Wine yeast	
Water to one gallon	4.5 litres

Remove any traces of decay from the apples, do not core or peel, simply chop the apples. Place in the bucket together with the blackberries and sugar. Cover with four pints (2.25 litres) of boiling water and allow to cool to fermenting temperature. Add the yeast and pectic enzyme, cover and stir daily. After seven days strain the liquid and transfer to the demijohn. Fit an airlock. Make up to one gallon after a further week of fermentation. Allow to work out until the wine is DRY. The resultant wine, which can be sweetened to taste, is light in body and deep rose in colour.

Bramble Tip Wine The growing tips are a bonus from this plant which is probably the finest of all our many winemaking ingredients. Pick only the first two inches (5 cm) of the growing plant. These should readily burst when squeezed between the fingers.

1 quart of bramble tips	1.25 litres
½ lb raisins	250 gms
½ lb prunes	250 gms
2 lbs sugar	900 gms
2 tsp citric acid	
Pectic enzyme	
Wine yeast	
Water to 1 gallon	4.5 litres

Mash the soft tips with a fork. Mince the raisins and soak the prunes. Discard the soaking water and place the prunes, raisins, bramble tips and sugar in the bucket. Cover with half a gallon (2.25 litres) of boiling water, add cold water to one gallon. Add the pectic enzyme, citric acid and wine yeast at 70°F (21°C). Stir daily and strain after seven days. Transfer to a demijohn.

Bullace The bullace is not a common fruit of the hedgerows, but it is well worth seeking out to make a medium sweet wine.

4 lb bullaces	1800 gms
1 lb crushed wheat	450 gms
3¼ lb sugar	1460 gms
Pectic enzyme	
Amylase	
Wine yeast	
Water to one gallon	4.5 litres

Wait until the bullaces have fully ripened before harvesting. Cut the fruit so as to reveal the stone, and place in the bucket with the crushed wheat. Add only three pounds (1350 gms) of the sugar and four pints (2.25 litres) of boiling water. Allow to cool, provide the liquid with both enzymes and the yeast; cover the bucket and allow to stand for ten days, after which time the liquid is strained and transferred to a demijohn. After the first racking make up the volume with remaining sugar dissolved in sufficient water to fill the demijohn. Drink the wine when it is clear.

Crab Apples The sugars are not fully developed in crab apples until the middle of November, and unless you delay the gathering of the fruit the resulting wine will be sharp to the taste.

5 lb crab apples	2250 gms
2½ lb sugar	1125 gms
Pectic enzyme	
Wine yeast	
Water to one gallon	4.5 litres

Examine the apples, discarding any that are decayed. Cut up as small as is practical and place in the bucket and add the sugar and five pints (3 litres) of boiling water. Allow to cool, add the yeast and enzyme. Stir the liquid daily, attempting to break up further the fruit as it softens. Allow the mixture to ferment for a fortnight and then strain into the demijohn. The resulting wine is a light dry table style, that may be sweetened immediately prior to serving.

Elderberry Wine The elder has been described as the vine of England and this is not surprising when you consider the quality of drink that both the fruit and the flowers produce. Elderberries are far too low in acid to make a wine without the addition of an extra acid-providing ingredient. To obtain a really quality wine you should use pure grapefruit juice to make up the difference. The old method of making elderberries was to ferment the juice in the presence of the fruit. Using this method the initially formed alcohol extracts too much tannin which resulted in a wine that is too harsh and requires years to mature.

Dry Elderberry Wine

2 lb elderberries	900 gms
1 litre pure grapefruit juice	1 litre
3 lb sugar	1350 gms
Pectic enzyme	
Wine yeast	
Water to one gallon	4.5 litres

It is a time-consuming task to strip the berries from the stalks but if you allow any of the green material to enter the bucket the wine will be spoilt. Place the stripped berries in the bucket and pound with a potato masher or fork. Add two pints of boiling water (1.25 litres) and allow the mixture to stand until it is cool enough to handle. Strain into a second bucket containing the sugar. Stir to dissolve the majority of the sugar, add the grapefruit juice. Check the temperature at 65-70°F (18.5-21°C); add the yeast and pectic enzyme. Keep in the bucket until the high frothy head subsides, then transfer to a demijohn without further straining. Fit an airlock. After one week add any additional water required. Ferment to dryness.

Sweet Elderberry Wine

2½ lb elderberries	1125 gms
1 lb raisins	450 gms
7 oz can of gooseberries	200 gms
3 lb sugar	1350 gms
Pectic enzyme	
Wine yeast	
Water to one gallon	4.5 litres

Extract the elderberry juice as described in the recipe above and transfer to a fermenting bucket, add the tin of gooseberries together with the juice that the can contains and the chopped raisins. Dissolve 2½ pounds (1125 gms) of the sugar in 2 pints (1.25 litres) of water and add these to the mixture. Check the temperature, at 65-70°F (18.5-21°C) add the yeast and pectic enzymes. After a fortnight strain and transfer to a demijohn make up to one gallon (4.5 litres) with tap water. After the first racking add a quarter of a pound (100 gms) of sugar dissolved in the water used for topping up. Add the same quantity after the second racking. This is a full-bodied wine of similar style to a port. If the wine is not sweet enough sugar syrup, to taste, may be added at any stage.

Hawthorn Wine Gathered after the first frost the berries of the hawthorn or May tree can be used to make a medium bodied wine.

3 lb hawthorn berries	1350 gms
3¼ lb sugar	1460 gms
2 tsp citric acid or the juice of two lemons	
Wine yeast	

Water to one gallon   4.5 litres

Clean the berries, pound and place in the fermenting bucket. Add three pounds of the sugar (1350 gms) and the citric acid or lemons, together with four pints (2.25 litres) of boiling water followed by two of cold. Check the temperature and add the yeast (pectic enzyme is not required with this fruit). After one week strain into a demijohn, add the extra quarter of a pound of sugar at the time of the first racking. Drink when clear.

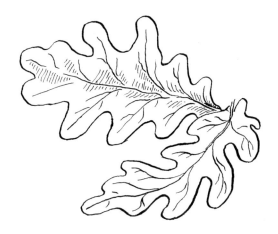

Oak Leaf Wine Use only the new, tender oak leaves and strip them from the twigs.

one quart of oak leaves	1.25 litre
2 lbs bananas	900 gms
2½ lbs sugar	1125 gms
2 tsp citric acid	
Wine yeast	
Water to 1 gallon	4.5 litres

Use over ripe bananas, peel and remove any decayed parts. Mash thoroughly with a fork and place in the bucket with the oak leaves. Cover with boiling water. Dissolve the sugar in the remaining water, and add the yeast and citric acid at 70°F (21°C). Allow to stand on the must for a fortnight, then place in a demijohn. This is a medium wine. It can be made into a sweet wine by adding a solution of ¼ lb (120 gms) of sugar dissolved in ½ pint (0.25 litre) of water at the racking stage.

Rose Hip Wine Only use wild rose hips and gather after the first frost.

3 lb rose hips	1350 gms
2½ lb white sugar	1125 gms
½ lb demerara sugar	225 gms
2 tsp citric acid or the juice of two lemons	
Wine yeast	
Water to one gallon	4.5 litres

Pound the rose hips to break them up. Then place in the bucket together with both types of sugar and the citric acid or the juice of two lemons. Add six pints of boiling water. Allow to cool, add the yeast (pectic enzyme is not required) and ferment in the bucket for a fortnight. Strain, transfer to a demijohn and fit an airlock. Add any additional water after one week. Taste after each racking, if the wine is not sweet enough add an extra quarter of a pound (100 gms) of sugar and ferment out. This process can be repeated until the correct degree of sweetnes is obtained.

Rowan (Mountain Ash) Berry Wine Like the hawthorn, the berries of the rowan tree can be used to make a very economical wine. Pick the fruit during the middle of October, but do not delay the harvest too long or the birds will have eaten all of the fruit. Use the same quantities and method as given for HAWTHORN WINE.

Sloe Wine For a really good sloe wine you must gather the fruits late, when the acid is at a minimum and the sugar has reached a maximum.

3 lb sloes	1350 gms
3 lb sugar	1350 gms
1 lb bananas	450 gms
Pectic enzyme	
Yeast	
Water to one gallon	4.5 litres

Gather the sloes and leave them to stand in the deep freeze compartment of the refrigerator for one week – this helps to break the fruit down. Place the fruit in the bucket together with the peeled bananas, again use only very ripe fruit. Cover with four pints (2.25 litres) of boiling water, dissolve in the sugar and add a pint (500 ml) of cold water. At 65-70°F (18.5-21°C) add the yeast and pectic enzyme. Stir daily. After seven days strain and transfer to the demijohn. A week later add any additional water. Should the wine retain any excess acidity add sugar syrup to taste immediately prior to serving.

Chapter Six

Fruit Wines

Depending upon the variety, fruit can provide flavour, acid and sugar to a wine. Some of the best wines can be made from the cheapest types of fruit, and since the riper that the fruit is the better will be the quality of the drink, you may buy over-ripe fruit at a reduced price and get an even better product. Whenever you use over-ripe fruit ensure that you remove any signs of decay, if left these would give the wine a musty taste.

Apple & Raisin Wine The type of wine that you obtain from apples will depend upon the time at which they were gathered – from September onwards fallers are ideal – the variety and the degree of breaking up of the fruit that you achieve.

4 lb apples	1800 gms
½ lb raisins	225 gms
2¾ lb sugar	1250 gms
Wine yeast	
Water to one gallon	4.5 litres

When preparing the must the aim should be to provide as much of the liquid as possible from the apples themselves. This can be achieved with either certain types of fruit presses or passing through a mincer and trapping the slurry, or failing this simply dicing the fruit. Chop the raisins and add to the apple in the bucket, add three pints (1.75 litres) of boiling water and dissolve the sugar in the liquid. Check the volume and if the total liquid appears to be below six pints (3.5 litres) add a further pint (500 ml) of tap water. At 65-70°F (18.5-21°C) add the yeast and ferment the mixture in the bucket for a fortnight. Strain into a demijohn and immediately top up with water. The wine develops a golden to tawny colour and it may be sweetened to taste.

Banana Wine Whenever bananas are used for winemaking, always buy those which appear to be over-ripe, with a black coloured skin. At this stage the banana will have commenced a series of chemical changes which greatly improve its vinification characteristics.

3 lb very ripe bananas	1350 gms
2¾ lb sugar	1250 gms
1 cup cold tea	
2 tsp citric acid or the juice of two lemons	
Wine yeast	
Water to one gallon	4.5 litres

Peel the bananas and discard the skins. Mash with a fork and place in the fermenting vessel together with the cold tea and citric acid. Add four pints (2.25 litres) of boiling water and two (1.25 litres) of cold. Check the temperature and when it is low enough add the yeast. Strain and put into a demijohn seven days later. A delay in straining can result in the wine possessing too strong a flavour. Rack in the usual way. The bananas themselves will contribute some sugar, so although the added sugar is quite low the wine should finish medium sweet. Extra sugar may be fed or added prior to serving, if required. No enzyme is included in this recipe as bananas seldom form a haze, but if the wine does not clear add amylase to counter any starch present. Generally clearing problems only occur if under-ripe fruit is used. This is such an easy wine to clear that some winemakers believe that the addition of bananas helps to clear a wine.

Blackberry and Banana Wine

3½ lb blackberries	1575 gms
¾ lb sultanas	336 gms
½ lb ripe bananas	225gms
3 lb sugar	1350 gms
Pectic enzyme	
Yeast	
Water to one gallon	4.5 litres

Peel the bananas and discard the skins, mash and place in the bucket together with the blackberries which should also be crushed with a fork. Chop the bananas and add the sugar. Add six pints (3.5 litres) of boiling water and when safe to handle stir to ensure that the sugar has completely dissolved. Cool to 65-70°F (18.5-21°C), add both the yeast and pectic enzyme. Stir daily, allow to remain in the bucket for 4 days (no longer, irrespective of the head, as the tannin content may be too high or the banana flavour may predominate). Transfer to a demijohn but do not top up as the liquid may 'creep up' through the airlock that should be fitted at this stage. After a further fortnight top up with tap water. Finish the wine in the usual way. This wine is best drunk between a month and two years, it may be sweetened to taste.

Blackcurrant Wine For a light dry red table wine with a very pleasant bouquet and taste you will require

2 lb blackcurrants	900 gms
2¾ lb sugar	1250 gms
¾ tsp citric acid	
Wine yeast	
Water to one gallon	4.5 litres

Remove the blackcurrants from the stalks but do not top and tail. Place in the bucket with the sugar and four pints (2.25 litres) boiling water. When the sugar has dissolved add a further two pints (1.25 litres) of tap water. Allow to cool, add the yeast and the citric acid. Stir daily, attempting to break open any fruit which have remained whole. After one week strain and gently squeeze. Top up the demijohn with water immediately. The wine which has a very fresh fruity taste should be drunk immediately that it has cleared.

Damson & Banana Wine The fresh taste of the damson adds a sharpness to the wine that gives it a particular clean and pleasant taste.

2 lb damsons	900 gms
2 lb bananas (weight including skins)	900 gms
2½ lb sugar (white)	1125 gms
½ lb sugar (demerara)	225 gms
Wine yeast	
Water to one gallon	4.5 litres

Cut or break the skins of the damsons and place together with the skinned bananas in the bucket. Break up both the fruits thoroughly with a fork and add the 2½ pounds (1125 gms) of white sugar. Cover with four pints (2.25 litres) of boiling water and dissolve the sugar. Add a further two pints (1.25 litres) of cold water, check the temperature and add the yeast. Ferment on the fruit daily and strain after seven days. Do not delay as after this period taste begins to be extracted from the stones of the fruit. Top up the level of the liquid and fit an airlock. Add half the demerara sugar as a syrup at the time of the first racking and the remainder after the second racking.

Japonica Wine Japonica wine is another bonus wine; during the spring and throughout the summer the plant is covered in deep pink flowers, and the quince-like fruits which change from green to yellow during autumn and winter are edible. These fruits, together with cloves, can be used to make a very tasty jelly, alternatively they may be used to make good medium sweet wine.

3 lb late gathered quinces	1350 gms
1 lb sultanas	450 gms
2½ lb sugar	1125 gms
2 tsp citric acid or tartaric acid	
Pectic enzyme	
Wine yeast	
Water to one gallon	4.5 litres

Wait until the quinces have turned a deep yellow colour; at this stage they will have developed brown 'freckles' on the skin. This is quite normal and it is not a sign of decay, although if any obvious decay is present it should be removed otherwise the wine will develop an 'earthy' taste. Quinces are hard fruit, with very little juices and their main contribution is flavour. To ensure that the maximum flavour can be extracted, chop the fruit as finely as is practical. Do not be tempted to bring the quinces to the boil as they contain a fairly high quantity of pectin and pectic enzyme does not always remove it completely, and you can end up with a hazy wine. Place the chopped fruit and the sultanas in the bucket, cover with four pints (2.25 litres) of boiling water. Allow to stand for twenty minutes, stir in the sugar and the acid and provide a further two pints (1.25 litres) of tap water. At 65-70°F (18.5-21°C) add the yeast and enzyme, STIR DAILY (important); after eight days strain and transfer to the demijohn, fit an airlock. There is insufficient acid and body for the wine to carry extra sweetness, so top up with water after racking. The wine matures after six months and will keep for a further year.

Orange Wine Oranges are best used to make a light dry table wine that retains its characteristic orange taste. As with all light wines it is best to drink them immediately that they are clear in order that they retain their freshness.

5 large oranges	
½ lb sultanas	225 gms
2½ lb sugar	1125 gms
Wine yeast	
Water to one gallon	4.5 litres

Peel the oranges, break into segments taking care to remove all traces of the white pith that adheres to the quarters. If any of this pith is allowed to enter the wine it will cause the drink to become bitter. Pound the segments with a potato masher and add the chopped sultanas together with the sugar. Cover with three pints (1.75 litres) of boiling water, dissolve the sugar and add a further two pints (1.25 litres) of cold water. Add the yeast when the temperature has dropped. Strain the solid after five days, transfer to a demijohn, top up with tap water and fit an airlock. Often this wine requires only one racking, drink when clear.

Peach Wine You will require:

6 large peaches	
½ lb sultanas	225 gms
3 lb sugar	1350 gms
Wine yeast	
Water to one gallon	4.5 litres

Remove the stones from the fruit, chop the sultanas, add the sugar followed by four pints (2.25 litres) of boiling water and two of cold. At 65-70°F (18.5-21°C) add the yeast, stir daily and leave in the bucket for seven to ten days. Strain, squeeze the bag lightly. Transfer to a demijohn and top up immediately. This is a medium wine, which should be drunk fairly young to retain the delicate flavour of the peaches.

Plum Wine This wine when finished has a flavour far removed from that of the original fruit, it is at its best if fed with extra sugar or served with sugar syrup.

4 lb plums	1800 gms
2 lb bananas	900 gms
2¾ lb sugar	1250 gms
Pectic enzyme	
Wine yeast	
Water to one gallon	4.5 litres

Remove all the stones from the plums, if they are allowed to remain they may give a woody 'off' flavour. Peel the bananas and discard the skins. Place two and a half pounds (1125 gms) of sugar in the fermenting bucket together with the fruit, add 5 pints (3 litres) of boiling water. Allow to cool and add the yeast and pectic enzyme (the use of enzymes is particularly important with this type of wine as plums seem to form a pectic haze more readily than most fruit). Ferment on the fruit, stirring daily. Strain after seven to ten days. Transfer to the demijohn, topping up with tap water immediately. Feed the remaining sugar as a syrup after the first racking. The wine when finished is medium sweet.

Raspberry Wine Raspberries alone tend to yield a thin wine, but since they have a strong flavour you may include up to two pounds of ripe bananas per gallon if you wish.

3 lb raspberries	1350 gms
2 lb bananas (optional)	900 gms
3 lb sugar	1350 gms
Wine yeast	
Water to one gallon	4.5 litres

Leave the fruit in the deep freeze for a week to help the breakdown and release of the juices. Place the raspberries in the bucket, and the peeled bananas if you intend using them. Cover with 4 pints (2.25 litres) of boiling water and add all the sugar. If you are incorporating bananas in the recipe add only two and three quarters pounds (1250 gms) of sugar and add the remainder as a syrup after the first racking. Provide a further pint of cold tap water. Check the temperature, when the liquid is sufficiently cool add the yeast. After seven days strain the liquid and transfer to a demijohn and ferment until clear.

Strawberry Wine Correctly made strawberry wine, which has a light tawny colour, will retain the characteristic taste and flavour of the fruit for several months. The strawberries themselves contain no body-producing materials and to make a worthwhile wine it is necessary to include a pound of sultanas in the recipe. It is best drunk as a medium wine.

3 lb strawberries	1350 gms
1 lb sultanas	450 gms
2½ lb sugar	1125 gms
½ tsp citric acid	
Wine yeast	
Water to one gallon	4.5 litres

Leave the strawberries in the deep freeze for a week if possible, this will cause the fruit to break down and release much of the juice, the process being completed by crushing in the bucket. Mince or chop the sultanas and add together with the sugar, to the strawberries. Pour three pints (1.75 litres) of boiling water on to the fruit and use this to dissolve the sugar. Add a further two pints (1.25 litres) of cold water. Allow to stand until the temperature has reached 65-70°F (18.5-21°C). Add the yeast and citric acid, ferment on the fruit for ten days, strain, top up immediately and fit an airlock. Taste the wine at the time of racking, if it is too dry for your taste feed with a further quarter of a pound of sugar as a syrup.

White Currant Wine White currants make probably the finest of all sweet white country wines.

4 lb white currants	1800 gms
3 lb sugar	1350 gms
Wine yeast	
Water to one gallon	4.5 litres

Remove the fruit from the stalks but do not top and tail them. Crush the fruit in the bucket. Add the sugar. Simultaneously dissolve the sugar and sterilise by adding five pints (3 litres) of boiling water. Do not add any extra water at this stage as the fruit often provides a large quantity of juice. Allow to cool. Add the yeast. Stir daily and leave the liquid to ferment for a fortnight. Strain, transfer to a demijohn and top up. Fit an airlock. It is not possible to know how sweet an individual wine is due to the variations in fruit sugar. If after the first racking the wine is not sweet enough feed an extra quarter of a pound of sugar as syrup.

Chapter Seven

Flower Wines

Flowers contribute only flavour and bouquet to a wine, but since even with ageing the substances that are responsible for the delicate bouquet of a flower hardly change, wines to which a small amount of flower petals have been added are invariably more appetising than those which have had no such additions.

For years flower wines have simply been flavoured sultana or raisin wines. Whilst these wines are well worth making, and recipes are included, it is possible to combine flowers with other basic winemaking ingredients, yielding cheaper and often better drinks than those using solely dried grapes. Such combinations are restricted by the failure of the seasons of the various ingredients to overlap.

When collecting flowers always smell the flowers first, as it is the bouquet of the flowers themselves that will give the character to the finished wine. Should you decide that you do not fancy a particular bouquet to the wine, then do not make that flower wine as it will not change with keeping.

The two most common mistakes made when preparing flower wines are the tendency to use too many flowers – use less rather than more than the stated quantity – and the inclusion of green pieces of plant material in the must, which will give the wine a bitter taste.

CAUTION Theoretically it is possible to make a wine using any garden or wild flowers. Most flowers are not poisonous, including the honeysuckle, whose berries are very dangerous, but it is not known which flowers have an ill effect and you should not try experimenting with any blossoms that you do not know to be safe.

Dandelion Wine This is another of the very old style country wines, which was usually made with raisins.

2	pints dandelion heads	1.25 litres
1	lb raisins	450 gms
2	Oranges	
2½	lb sugar	1125 gms
	Wine yeast	
	Water to one gallon	4.5 litres

Measure two pints (1.25 litres) of loosely packed heads, pull the flowers from the stalks and the green surrounds. Peel the oranges, removing all traces of the white pith from the segments which are then placed in the bucket and crushed. Chop the raisins and add to the oranges, flowers and sugar. Cover with three pints (1.75 litres) of water, stir thoroughly and add the same volume of cold water. Allow the temperature to drop to 65-70°F (18.5-21°C). After ten days strain into the demijohn and fit an airlock. Most raisins contain a fairly high proportion of sugar and the finished wine should be medium sweet. If required the sweetness may be increased by feeding or adding sugar syrup immediately prior to serving.

Elderflower Wine

6 elderflower heads	
1 lb sultanas	450 gms
2¾ lb sugar	1250 gms
2 tsp citric acid or the juice of	
two lemons	
Wine yeast	
Water to one gallon	4.5 litres

Select six medium sized flower heads with the blossom fully open. Place in a plastic bag and shake thoroughly to dislodge the petals. Remove the stalks and use only the white petals and the yellow pollen. Add the chopped sultanas to the elderflower, citric acid (or the juice from two lemons) and two pints (1.25 litres) of boiling water followed half an hour later by a further four pints (2.25 litres) of cold water. The yeast may be added immediately. Stir daily, when the initial head subsides strain the liquid into a demijohn, fit an airlock and ferment until the wine is clear.

Elderflower & Banana Wine Elderflowers and bananas have a similar bouquet and the two ingredients compliment each other.

6 elderflower heads	
2 lb bananas	900 gms
3 lb sugar	1350 gms
2 tsp citric acid or the juice of	
two lemons	
1 cup cold tea	
Wine yeast	
Water to one gallon	4.5 litres

Collect the blooms and separate the flowers and the pollen as described in the previous recipe. Place all the ingredients except the yeast in the fermenting bucket. Add two pints (1.25 litres) of boiling water and dissolve the sugar and follow with a further four pints (2.25 litres) of cold water. Provide the yeast when cool. Strain and place in a demijohn after one week. The degree of sweetness will depend upon the sugar in the bananas. Taste the wine after the first racking and if it is not sweet enough add a further quarter of a pound of sugar as syrup. Ferment until clear.

Honeysuckle & Pea Pod Wine Pea pods provide a wine with body but very little flavour. Combined with honeysuckle they yield a cheap full-bodied wine that has the unmistakable bouquet of one of the most pleasant of all the flowers of the countryside.

3 lb pea pods	1350 gms
1 pint honeysuckle flowers	500 ml
3 lb sugar	1350 gms
2 tsp citric acid or the juice of two lemons	
Wine yeast	
Water to one gallon	4.5 litres

Wash the pea pods, and remove the green material from the flowers. Place in the bucket with the sugar and citric acid or lemon juice. Cover with 3 pints (1.75 litres) of boiling water, some of the pods will float but the sterilisation will still be effective. Add a further 3 pints of cold water and check the temperature. Leave the liquid to ferment on the solid for ten days, strain, transfer to the demijohn and finish the wine in the usual way.

Marigold Wine Use the large headed varieties of marigold, employing the petals pulled from the base of the flowers.

¾ pint marigold heads	375 ml
1 lb raisins	450 gms
2¾ lb sugar	1250 gms
3 tsp citric acid or the juice of three lemons	
Wine yeast	
Water to one gallon	4.5 litres

Add only two and a half pounds (1125 gms) sugar to the flower heads and chopped raisins, at this stage retaining the remainder for feeding at the racking stage. Cover with four pints (2.25 litres) of boiling water dividing the sugar in the process. Stir daily, leave for a fortnight, transfer to the demijohn and top up. The time that the wine takes to clear will depend upon the type of raisins used, but normally it will have clarified by the time of the second racking. Just occasionally certain types of raisin will give a slight haze, this readily clears if treated with a proprietary wine fining agent.

Rose Petal Wine The quantity of rose petals that you require will depend upon the degree of perfume that occurs in the variety used. For heavily scented varieties use only one pint per gallon,with more subtle species double this quantity.

1-2 pints rose petals	0.5-1 litre
1 litre of grapefruit juice	
½ lb sultanas	225 gms
3 lb sugar	1350 gms
Wine yeast	
Water to one gallon	4.5 litres

Ensure that you do not spray roses whose flowers you wish to use for winemaking. Gather the petals after the flowers have fully opened and the petals come away readily in the hand. Place the petals, chopped sultanas and sugar in the bucket. Add three pints (1.75 litres) of boiling water and allow to cool. At 65-70°F (18.5-21°C) add the pure grapefruit juice and the wine yeast. Stir daily. Many rose petals turn brown in colour, this will not adversely affect the wine. Allow the rose petals to remain in the liquid until the vigorously fermenting head has subsided. Strain into a demijohn, top up and ferment until the wine has clarified.

Wallflower Wine Wallflowers with their distinctive bouquet can be used to flavour either a raisin or sultana wine, but since they are in season at the same time as rhubarb the two together produce a top-quality wine very cheaply.

1 pint wallflowers	0.5 litres
3 lb rhubarb	1350 gms
3 lb sugar	1350 gms
Wine yeast	
Water to one gallon	4.5 litres

Use only the flowering parts of the wallflower. Peel the rhubarb and cut into pieces about two to three inches (5-8 cms) long. Place in the bucket with the sugar. Since the rhubarb is skinned it will be free from any infection and flowers do not tend to harbour wild yeasts. The cold water soak is a better method with rhubarb. Dissolve the sugar in 2 pints (1.25 litres) of hot water and 4 of cold, allow to cool and add to the wallflowers and rhubarb. Add the yeast. Leave for a fortnight. Do not stir. Strain, transfer to a demijohn and top up as necessary.

Chapter Eight

Vegetable Wines

Legends abound concerning the strength of homemade wine and few enjoy a better reputation in this respect than the root wines. In truth a parsnip wine is no stronger than a blackberry, but the slight burning sensation that they give at the back of the throat certainly makes them seem very strong, which of course all country wines are. Once the quality of country wines was realised the search began for other garden produce that might be used for drink making. Most plants have now been tried and it is possible to find recipes quoted for virtually everything that grows in the vegetable plot. However only a small percentage of them yield an acceptable wine.

Beetroot Wine Beetroot wine is not, as might be expected, a deep red, but rather a tawny that some people consider bears a resemblance to Port.

4 lb beetroot	1800 gms
3½ lb sugar	1575 gms
2½ tsp citric acid or 2 large lemons	
Wine yeast	
Water to one gallon	4.5 litres

Do not peel the beetroot but scrub the roots to ensure that no dirt remains. Dice the beetroot and cover immediately with 4 pints (2.25 litres) of boiling water. When cool enough to handle stir in three pounds of the sugar and add the acid or lemon juice. Add a further 2 pints (1.25 litres) of cold water and check the temperature. At 65-70°F (18.5-21°C), add the yeast. Stir daily. After ten days dissolve a quarter of a pound of sugar in a quarter of a pint of water and add this to the strainings in the demijohn. If the wine is dry after the first racking add the remainder of the sugar. Should the wine remain sweet, delay the addition of sugar until such time as it is dry. Do not keep this wine for more than eighteen months, after which time it slowly begins to acquire an earthy taste.

Carrot Wine Many variations exist of the traditional country wine often called carrot whisky.

3 lb carrots	1350 gms
3 medium sized oranges	
½ lb raisins	225 gms
3 lb sugar	1350 gms
Wine yeast	
Water to one gallon	4.5 litres

Boil the peeled carrots until they are soft. Transfer the vegetables together with the liquid into the fermenting bucket. Chop the raisins and add with the sugar. Remove the skin and ALL traces of white pith from the oranges, place in the bucket and break up with a fork. Add six pints (3.5 litres) of lukewarm water, stir thoroughly to dissolve the sugar then add the yeast. Stir daily, ensuring that the orange segments are completely broken up. Strain after seven days into a demijohn, top up and fit an airlock. Should the wine not clarify within nine months add a proprietary fining agent, if this does not prove successful,

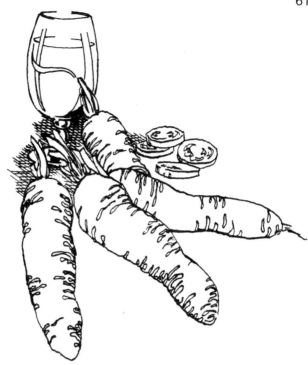

then add amylase. Usually the wine presents few problems. It is best drunk dry.

Mangold & Turnip Wines The most difficult characteristic to obtain in a wine is body, and this can often be obtained from the materials contained in roots. Consequently the old country winemakers used roots which were always available, usually at no cost to them, to make their wines. Both turnips and mangolds have the same effect upon the must and a similar recipe can be employed for both roots.

4	lb either turnips or mangolds	1800 gms
2	tsp citric acid	
1	lb raisins	450 gms
3	lb white sugar	1350 gms
	Amylase	
	Wine yeast	
	Water to one gallon	4.5 litres

To avoid an earthy taste in the wine peel the roots, then chop and place in a saucepan with sufficient water to cover. Bring to the boil and pour both the liquid and the solid into the bucket. Add the raisins, sugar and citric acid then cover with four pints (2.25 litres) of boiling water. Cover the liquid and allow to cool to 65-70°F (18.5-21°C), add the yeast and amylase. Stir daily. After the vigorous yeast head has subsided strain the liquid immediately and transfer to a demijohn. Top up with water if necessary. The wine will ferment down to medium sweet, extra sugar syrup may be added if desired. Such a wine will develop 14-15% alcohol and is not at its best until it is a year old.

Marrow Wine The original method of making marrow wine was to take a medium sized marrow and cut in two halves length-wise. The seeds were scooped out, the cavity filled with brown sugar and the two halves tied together. A hole was then bored into the base of the marrow and the liquid allowed to drip out. The resultant liquid was very sweet, and kept almost indefinitely. Although the drink contains very little alcohol the brown sugar gives a characteristic taste which reminds many people of rum and hence the country name of the drink – marrow rum.

Far superior to this very variable drink is the wine made from the following

1 medium-size marrow	
2 lb white sugar	900 gms
1 lb demerara sugar	450 gms
2 tsp citric acid or juice from 2 lemons	
Wine yeast	
Water to one gallon	4.5 litres

Ensure that you use a fully ripe marrow. Peel the marrow, remove the seeds, then cut the vegetable into large chunks. Cover the marrow with the white sugar and half of the demerara, followed by four pints (2.25 litres) of boiling water. Add the citric acid or the juice of the lemons and provide two pints (1.25 litres) of cold water. Stir to ensure that the sugar has dissolved and add the yeast at 65-70°F (18.5-21°C). Break up the marrow as you stir the liquid daily. After seven days strain, transfer to the demijohn and top up. After the first racking add half of the remaining demerara sugar dissolved in warm water, add the rest at the time of the second racking.

Parsnip & Orange Wine Parsnip wine has been made for years with just the addition of an orange and lemon to provide the acid and a little extra body and flavour. By employing orange juice in preference to the fruit there is a very pronounced improvement in the finished product.

3 lb parsnips	1350 gms
1 litre carton of orange juice	
1 tsp citric acid	
3 lb white sugar	1350 gms
½ lb sultanas	225 gms
Wine yeast	
Water to one gallon	4.5 litres

Cut the scrubbed, but not peeled, parsnip and bring to the boil with three pints (1.75 litres) of water. Simmer until the vegetables are soft. Pour the hot liquid on to the chopped sultanas. Dissolve the sugar in two pints (1.25 litres) of water and add this together with the orange juice. Parsnips contain large quantities of starch and it is essential that amylase is added with the yeast at 65-70°F (18.5-21°C) if a hazy wine is to be avoided. Allow the liquid to ferment for ten days then strain into a demijohn and top up with water if necessary. This wine is slower to mature than many and it should not be drunk until it is at least one year old.

Potato Wine The old method of making potato wine consisted of fermenting together two or three potatoes, a similar number of apples, an orange and some sugar. Such a blend of fruit and vegetables occasionally yielded a good wine, but more frequently the results were disappointing. A more modern recipe is given below; this retains the essential characteristic of a typical potato wine but produces a good quality drink every time. It can be made at any time of the year.

1 lb potatoes	450 gms
1 litre apple juice	
1½ tsp citric acid	
1 lb raisins	450 gms
3 lb sugar	1350 gms
Amylase	
Wine yeast	
Water to one gallon	4.5 litres

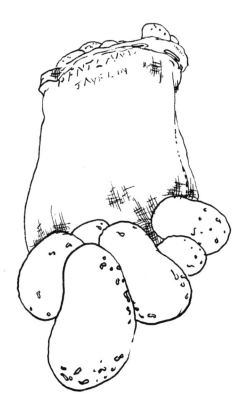

Peel the potatoes and chop the raisins, then place both in a bucket. Cover with four pints (2.25 litres) of boiling water. When cool add 2½ lb sugar (1125 gms) and four pints of boiling water. When the mixture is cool enough to handle stir to dissolve the sugar and allow the temperature to drop to 65-70°F (18.5-21°C). Add the apple juice, citric acid and yeast. As the potatoes have not been boiled very little starch will have been released and a haze seldom results. Amylase may be omitted at this stage. Should the wine fail to clear completely then the enzyme may be added after fermentation is complete. Although it is not as active in the presence of alcohol, it is effective enough to remove any slight traces formed as a result of the mild treatment of the potatoes employed in this recipe. Allow the wine to ferment on the solid until the vigorous fermentation has subsided – 5-10 days according to the temperature – then strain the liquid and transfer to the demijohn. After two months rack the wine and top up with a quarter of a pound (100 gms) of sugar dissolved in sufficient water to fill the air space. Repeat this procedure when a further quarter of an inch (½ cm) of sludge has formed. Apple juice oxidises very readily and acquires a brown tinge, this together with the colouring matter in the raisins results in a tawny coloured wine that often possesses some of the characteristics of a sweet sherry.

Rhubarb Wine Rhubarb wine is the country wine 'par excellence' and has all the characteristics that are expected in this style of drink. It is cheap, easy to make and it has a distinctive taste. Much nonsense is talked about the wine being poisonous. The rhubarb plant does contain a poison, oxalic acid, but it is only found in large quantities in the leaves. However as the stalks get older they do acquire more oxalic acid and whilst this will not be sufficient to be dangerous it will tend to make the wine over-acid. To avoid the problem always use young stalks to make the wine.

3 lb rhubarb stalks	1350 gms
3 lb sugar	1350 gms
1 cup cold tea	
Wine yeast	
Water to one gallon	4.5 litres

Chop the stalks into pieces about 2 inches long (5 cms) but do not peel. Place in the bucket together with the sugar dissolved in three pints of hot water. Add three pints (1.75 litres) of cold water, the yeast and cold tea. Cover the wine, check that fermentation has started after two days, uncover and leave completely undisturbed for a fortnight. If after this time a white film has formed, carefully remove with a spoon before straining. Should a white film fail to develop do not worry as this only occurs with varieties of rhubarb high in acid or when the stalks are getting old. After straining the rhubarb, which will be pulp-like in consistency, transfer to the demijohn, top up, fit an airlock and finish fermenting in the usual manner. Rhubarb wine is another wine best drunk dry although it can be sweetened to taste.

Tomato Wine Tomatoes are not an obvious ingredient for winemaking, and the wine that they yield – a dry aperitif style with a taste very reminiscent of herb wines – will not appeal to everyone, but they are wines of real character and I have known tomato wines to win in some of the best shows. Under no circumstances attempt to make a sweet tomato wine as the taste of tomato and sugar together will not appeal to many palates.

2 lb tomatoes	900 gms
2¾ lb sugar	1250 gms
2 tsp citric acid	
Wine yeast	
Water to one gallon	4.5 litres

Harvest the tomatoes when they are still a pale orange colour, slice into quarters and place into the bucket together with the sugar. Add four pints (2.25 litres) of boiling water and when cool dissolve the sugar by stirring. Add a further three pints (1.75 litres) of cold water, stir again to obtain an even temperature throughout, then immediately add the yeast. Allow the solids and liquids to remain together for a fortnight, then strain, transfer to the demijohn topping up if necessary with tap water. Under no circumstances should you provide extra sugar at the racking stage. The wine, which can be drunk as soon as it is clear, will continue to improve for up to two years.

Chapter Nine

Wines From Juices, Tins And Kits

Home winemaking began as an agreeable way of utilising the fruits of the garden and the free crops of the hedgerow, but urban man, no longer tied to the cycles of the seasons, has learnt to make wines from convenience foods, and top of the lists are canned fruits and fruit juices. Such ingredients have several advantages over the traditional winemaking materials.

Fruit juices are completely extracted, are easily obtained, and because of the method of extraction the juices are sterile and do not require treatment with boiling water. However, this highly effective extraction has the disadvantage that only limited quantities can be employed in a recipe, as virtually all the essences are present, and if large amounts are used the wine possesses an overpowering flavour. This restriction on the quantity of fruit that can be used means that the only wines that are really successful from these ingredients are the light table wines. Wines made from tinned fruits and juices are not expensive because of the relatively small quantities employed.

NOTE When making wines from fruit juices use only the pure juice. Under no circumstances should you try to ferment squashes as these contain preservatives which will kill the yeast.

Apple Juice Wine Apples make one of the finest of all light wines. providing that it does not turn to cider or that it is oxidised to a brown colour. Good winemaking techniques will ensure that neither of these problems spoil the finished wine. As an extra precaution a Campden tablet should be added to each gallon (4.5 litres) after the final racking.

2 litres apple juice	
3 lb sugar	1350 gms
Wine yeast	
1 Campden tablet	
Water to one gallon	4.5 litres

Due to the large volume of added fruit juice there will only be sufficient room to add about two pints (1.25 litres) of water. To avoid wastage ensure that all the sugar is dissolved in this volume of very hot water. (Sugar is not sufficiently soluble to readily form this strength solution with cold water.) Cool the syrup, then add to the apple juice and yeast in the fermentation bucket. When the initial fermentation has subsided transfer, without straining, to the fermentation jar, fit an airlock and finish in the usual manner, adding one crushed Campden tablet per gallon to the finished wine.

Blackcurrant, Blackberry & Damson Wine Providing that you use the correct fruits in the right amounts it appears that the greater the number of different ingredients that you employ the higher the quality of the wine. All of the fruits given in this recipe are readily available, but if you cannot obtain all three use any two doubling the quantity of one.

7-8	oz tin blackcurrants	200-250 gms
7-8	oz tin blackberries	200-250 gms
7-8	oz tin damsons	200-250 gms
½ lb sultanas		225 gms
1¾ lb sugar		775 gms
Pectic enzyme		
Wine yeast		
Water to one gallon		4.5 litres

Place the blackcurrants and blackberries together with their syrup into a fermenting bucket and break up the fruit with a potato masher, then add the damsons and syrup. Cut the sultanas and rapidly bring to the boil with a pint (0.5 litre) of water. Place a quart (1.25 litres) of cold water in the bucket to protect the fruit and then pour the sultanas and liquid into the fermenting vessel, dissolve the sugar in a pint to a pint and a half (0.93 litres) of hot water and add to the mixture. Allow the temperature to reach 65-70°F (18.5-21°C), add the yeast and pectic enzyme. Cover. After three days the stones usually separate from the damsons, when this has occurred strain or decant the liquid into a demijohn. Fit an airlock but do not top up at this stage. Should the stones have failed to separate after seven days strain the liquid through the muslin and transfer to the demijohn. After ten days top up with tap water. Rack when level of sediment is between ¼ and ⅛ of an inch (5mm). When fermentation is complete bottle and allow to mature for three months.

Dried Orange Blossom Flower Wine Home-brew shops and health food shops sell dried orange blossom flowers. These can be converted into wine at any time of the year. The recipe given below makes a particularly enjoyable aperitif.

½ oz dried orange blossom flowers	14 gms
1 lb raisins	450 gms
2½ lb sugar	1125 gms

    3 tsp citric acid or the juice of
    three lemons
Wine yeast
Water to one gallon   4.5 litres
Make the wine as described for marigold above, but omit the
extra sugar at the racking stage.

Grapefruit Wine Fresh grapefruit was one of the first of the
newer ingredients used for winemaking. Grapefruit juice apart
from saving work has the advantage that it is cheaper to use
than fresh fruit. Adding a can of fresh grape concentrate tends
to make this one of the most expensive homemade wines, but it
often bears a very close resemblance to commercial wines. To
fully appreciate this wine it should always be drunk whilst still
young and slightly chilled.

    1 litre of white grapefruit juice
    1 can white grape juice concentrate
    12 oz sugar   350 gms
    Wine yeast
    Water to one gallon   4.5 litres
As all the ingredients are sterile there is no need to treat with
boiling water, which could have adverse effects on some of the
very delicate essences that the manufacturers go to such
lengths to retain in the liquid. However it is essential that all
the equipment is rendered sterile. Slightly warm a pint and a
half of the water and dissolve the sugar. Add this liquid straight
into the demijohn, then provide the grapefruit juice and grape
juice concentrate. Use only sufficient concentrate to take the
total volume up to within three inches of the neck of the
demijohn. Add the yeast and fit an airlock. Allow the wine to
ferment under air until you are sure that the initial head has
subsided, then top up with water. If you add the topping up
liquid before the initial stage is complete, the wine will spill
over into the airlock. Ferment the wine until dry and then rack.
This is a delicate wine and in order to protect the brew, if you do
not intend drinking immediately, crush ONE Campden tablet and
add to the mixture before bottling.

Gooseberry Wine Should your idea of winemaking be to
produce a drink similar in style to those which you buy, you will

probably achieve the best results from a combination of gooseberries and grape juice. This is not a cheap wine to make, but it does possess quality.

14-16 oz tin of gooseberries	350-450 gms
2 litres grape juice	
2 lb white sugar	900 gms
1 Campden tablet	
Wine yeast	
Water to one gallon	4.5 litres

Dissolve the sugar in one pint (0.5 litres) of water and allow to cool in a covered bucket before adding the gooseberries and grape juice. Allow the mixture to remain in the bucket for five days before transferring to the demijohn. Strain, top up the demijohn and fit an airlock. To ensure that the wine possesses freshness it is essential that the fermentation is completed in the shortest possible time. This can be achieved by constantly maintaining the temperature at 70°F (21°C) or slightly higher, but do not allow the value to rise above 75°F (23°C). After racking add one crushed Campden tablet per gallon of water.

Mandarin Orange Wine

14-16 oz mandarins	350-450 gms
½ lb sultanas	
2½ lb sugar	1125 gms
2 tsp tartaric acid	
1 cup cold tea	
Wine yeast	
Water to one gallon	4.5 litres

Chop the sultanas and place in the fermentation bucket, cover with two pints (1.25 litres) of boiling water to sterilise the dried fruit. Stir in the sugar until dissolved, add the cold tea and tartaric acid. Pour in the mandarins and syrup. Then provide a further two pints (1.25 litres) of tap water. Check that the temperature is at 65-70°F (18.5-21°C), then add the yeast. Stir the liquid daily and retain in the bucket for ten to fourteen days. Strain and transfer to the demijohn. Top up and fit an airlock then ferment to medium dryness.

Mixed Fruit Wine It appears, in general, that the greater the variety of fruits that are used in any one gallon the higher the quality of the wine. The various mixed fruit juices that are available all make a very acceptable wine, especially if blended with bananas. From a winemaking standpoint these mixed fruit juices appear to be slightly low in acid, but the problem can be overcome by the addition of a small quantity of tartaric acid.

2 litres mixed fruit juice	
1½ lb bananas	675 gms
1 tsp tartaric acid	
3 lb sugar	1350 gms
Wine yeast	
Water to one gallon	4.5 litres

Peel the bananas, discard the skins, and place the fruit together with two pints (1.25 litres) of water in a saucepan. Bring to the boil and simmer for thirty minutes. Strain the liquid on to the sugar contained in a fermenting bucket, stir to dissolve, adding a small quantity of extra hot water if necessary. Discard the spent bananas. Cover the bucket and allow to cool to about 70°F (21°C), then add the fruit juice, tartaric acid and a quart (1.25 litres) of cold water followed by the yeast. After ten days transfer the liquid, which will not require straining, straight into the demijohn. Allow to ferment, racking as necessary until the escape of bubbles ceases. Then bottle.

Mixed Fruit Wine When making any mixed fruit wine the amount of acids present in the various types of fruit is critical, so resist the temptation to simply mix together any cans that are available and restrict yourself to this tried and tested recipe.

6-8 oz tin apricots	175-225 gms
6-8 oz tin plums	175-225 gms
6-8 oz tin grapefruit segments	175-225 gms
1¾ lb sugar	775 gms
1 cup cold tea	
Wine yeast	
Water to one gallon	4.5 litres

Dissolve the sugar in two pints (1.25 litres) of water, then place all the ingredients, including the yeast and cold tea, in the fermentation bucket. Stir daily. After seven to ten days strain the wine into the demijohn, top up and fit an airlock. Ferment to dryness. The resulting wine is a reasonably full-bodied style which you may prefer to sweeten slightly, in which case you are best advised to add sugar syrup to the bottles before serving. If you feed the wine with extra syrup the resulting brew may develop more alcohol than the drink can carry.

Morello Cherry Wine Certain styles of port, noticeably the rubies, carry a slight almond-like flavour. Although this particular wine lacks the port style, to achieve that it is necessary to perform other operations such as fortifying with brandy, it does possess certain characteristics that the port drinkers will find very agreeable.

6-8 oz tin Morello cherries	175-225 gms
1 tin full bodied red wine concentrate	
1 lb sugar	450 gms
Port wine yeast	
Water to one gallon	4.5 litres

Dissolve eight ounces of sugar in a pint (0.5 litres) of water. Place the syrup, the cherries and the syrup that they contain, and the wine concentrate in a bucket. Wash the concentrate can with water and add to the other ingredients including the yeast, together with two pints (1.25 litres) of tap water. After seven days transfer the liquid to the demijohn. After the first racking feed the wine by adding a quarter of a pound (100 gms) of sugar syrup dissolved in the top-up water. Repeat this procedure when the wine is racked for the second time. The wine should be racked finally when all signs of fermentation have ceased. Bottle after the final racking.

Orange Concentrate Wine Generally we try to develop vinosity – the character of the grape – in a wine; however, many winemakers like to retain some of the character of the ingredient. This can be achieved when making an orange wine by adding the zest of the fruit. Great care must be taken not to add any of the white material of the peel as this will result in the wine having a bitter taste.

1 can of white grape juice concentrate	
10 oz white sugar	280 gms
1 litre orange juice	
1 medium sized orange	
Wine yeast	
Water to one gallon	4.5 litres

It is unlikely that any of these ingredients will have wild yeasts associated with them so we can avoid the necessity of sterilising with boiling water. Dissolve the sugar in a small quantity of water. Grate the rind of the orange and place in a demijohn, then add the orange juice, grape juice concentrate, sugar syrup and sufficient water to bring the level of the liquid up to three inches (6cm) below the neck of the container. Put in a warm place, check the temperature and add the yeast. Maintain the temperature at 65-70°F (18.5-21°C). When there is no longer a danger of the liquid rising into the airlock, top up with tap water. Ferment to dryness.

Orange & Sultana Wine

1 litre pure orange juice	
1 lb light coloured sultanas	450 gms
2 lb sugar	900 gms
½ tsp citric or tartaric acid	
Pectic enzyme	
Wine yeast	
Water to one gallon	4.5 litres

Cut each of the sultanas in half, then place in a saucepan with a pint (0.5 litre) of water, bring RAPIDLY to the boil and IMMEDIATELY remove from the heat source. Pour the hot liquid and solid on to the sugar contained in the bucket and add a further pint (0.5 litre) of very hot water. Stir until all of the sugar has dissolved, add three pints (1.75 litres) of cold tap water, stir to distribute the heat and then add the orange juice. Check the temperature with a thermometer, when it has dropped to 65-70°F (18.5-21°C) add the yeast, pectic enzyme and acid, cover the fermentation bucket and stir daily. After seven days strain and transfer to a demijohn; fit an airlock. Allow to ferment to dryness. Unless you intend to drink the wine quickly protect with a Campden tablet followed by potassium sorbate.

Peach Wine Peaches are one of the few wines that retain the taste and flavour of the original fruit so unless you enjoy that taste of peaches, as many people do, you should avoid this wine. Because of the pronounced flavour the wine is best made as either a medium or full sweet style. Do not be tempted to use more than the recommended quantities of peaches.

7-8 oz peaches	200-250 gms
1 lb sultanas	450 gms
3 lb sugar	1350 gms
1 tsp citric acid	
Wine yeast	
Water to one gallon	4.5 litres

Place the sultanas in a bucket with two pints (1.25 litres) of water and bring just to the boil, then immediately remove from the heat and transfer to the fermentation bucket. Stir in 2½ lb (1125 gms) of the sugar, and dissolve adding extra water if necessary. Leave in a covered container, add the peaches and citric acid together with a further two and a half pints (1.5 litres) of water, then provide the yeast. Strain into the demijohn after ten days. Top up and fit an airlock. After racking add a further quarter of a pound of sugar dissolved in sufficient water to refill the demijohn. If you prefer a medium wine, bottle after the second racking. Where a sweet wine is being prepared top up after the second racking with a further quarter of a pound of sugar syrup dissolved in water. Medium wines are ready for drinking after six months and the sweeter variation after nine.

Peach and Apricot Wine Because of the variety of materials employed and the necessity to keep the cost within reasonable limits the following recipe was developed on the basis of a two gallon (9 litres) brew. It is impracticable to make smaller amounts.

1 can white grape juice concentrate	
16 oz tin of peaches	450 gms
16 oz tin apricots	450 gms
1 litre pure grapefruit juice	
4 lb sugar	1800 gms
2 tsp citric or tartaric acid	
Pectic enzyme	
Wine yeast	
Water to two gallons	9 litres

Place the tinned fruit together with their syrup in a bucket, mashing the fruit as far as it is possible and the concentrate and the washings from the can. Pour in the grapefruit juice. Add three pints (1.75 litres) of cold water, stir thoroughly. Dissolve the sugar in three pints (1.75 litres) of very hot water and add the syrup to that contained in the bucket. Again mix thoroughly, check the temperature and provide the yeast, acid and pectic enzyme. Stir daily. Strain and transfer to a demijohn, after seven days top up. Often this is clear and ready for drinking after one racking. If you do not intend to drink the wine quickly, and remember you will have two gallons (9 litres), protect by the addition of a Campden tablet followed by potassium sorbate.

Pineapple Wine The traces of pineapple bouquet and flavour that remain until the wine is drunk make this an interesting wine completely different in character from any that you can buy. When purchasing grape juice ensure that it is pure unconcentrated grape juice which can now be obtained from most supermarkets and health food stores.

1   litre pineapple juice
1   litre grape juice
2¾ lb sugar   1250 gms
1   tsp tartaric acid
Wine yeast
Water to one gallon   4.5 litres

Dissolve the sugar in two pints (1.25 litres) of hot water and allow the syrup to cool. Pour the syrup, pineapple juice and grape juice straight into the demijohn. Add the yeast when the temperature has dropped to 65-70°F (18.5-21°C) and fit an airlock. When you are sure that the initial voluminous head has subsided sufficiently to ensure that the liquid will not spill over into the airlock, top up with tap water. Rack when a half an inch (1 cm) of sediment has formed.

Wines From Tinned Fruit To the city dweller, who has to buy all his fruit for winemaking, tinned fruit is only slightly more expensive than the fresh variety. Due to the method of canning the extraction of flavour and other materials is far easier than with fresh fruit, consequently smaller quantities may be used. Fruits are canned in sugar syrup and this liquid should be added to the winemaking materials. The recommended amounts of sugar should be provided in addition to the quantities contained in the tin. There are slight variations in can sizes, but these differences will be insignificant in terms of the total amounts used, and you may safely purchase any can the contents of which lie within the given limits.

Wine Kits No book on winemaking would be complete without a consideration of kit wines. Kits come complete and require no additions except sugar, and even this is not necessary with certain brands. Yeast is supplied with many winemaking concentrates. All the problems of manufacturing the liquid from which the wine is to be brewed are solved for the kit winemaker. Although he will have to pay a little more for his drink, will have less of a variety and body – it is seldom possible to obtain the depth of body and character from kits that the country winemaker can achieve – winemaking from these cans is a far easier operation.

Today's wine kits are the liquid equivalent of a convenience food but, unlike other partially prepared products, the wine-maker has to conduct the fermentation, and this involves the living organism yeast. Wherever a living organism is involved there is always the possibility of problems arising. Such problems are easily overcome simply by following good wine-making techniques. Whilst the instructions provided by most concentrates stress the need for hygiene, most of the criticism levelled at these wines results from carelessness in this respect rather than poor compounding of the original kit. Many kit winemakers do not feel the need to read a winemaking book, or to understand the operations involved in preparing a wine. This leads to another common mistake of pouring wine from the demijohn, rather than from a bottle. The resultant air space is an open invitation for bacteria. This coupled with the lower alcohol level results in the wine having less inbuilt protection from attack, and a spoilt drink often follows.

KITS MAKE WINEMAKING AN EVEN SIMPLER PROCESS THAN COUNTRY WINEMAKING, BUT UNLESS YOU TAKE THE BASIC PRECAUTIONS YOU ARE NO MORE LIKELY TO MAKE A GOOD WINE FROM THESE INGREDIENTS THAN FROM ANY OTHER.

Chapter Ten

A Miscellany of Country Wines

The diversity of country wines is infinite. Visit any large agricultural show and you will find amongst the exhibits a whole range of wines. In addition to the familiar elderberry and blackberry will appear every type of flower, fruit and vegetable that you can imagine. Often you will hear a visitor expressing surprise and commenting along the lines that 'I did not know you could make wine from ...' In truth you can make wine from anything which is not poisonous. What the resultant drink will taste like is another matter! I have listed details of so many different types of wine that there should be no reason to wish to try others. Often the argument put forward is that a particular ingredient is free therefore it might just as well be converted into wine as wasted. Cheap home made wines may be, but free they are certainly not. In addition to the cost of sugar and additives such as sultanas there is the cost of chemicals, and most winemakers only have a limited number of demijohns. There are, however, several ingredients that appear to have little winemaking potential that have been used for this purpose for several years. The list includes grains, herbs and even saps, all of which produce wines that are not only excellent drinks in their own right but they are also conversation pieces.

Grain Wines Grains contribute flavour through their husks and there are materials within the seed itself which will build the body of a wine. Unfortunately also included in the grain are large quantities of starch which can cause a haze. To avoid this problem immediately after boiling water has been added (to sterilise the grains) cold water should be provided to make up the bulk and simultaneously lower the temperature. This minimises the period of time that the starch is subjected to the heat treatment which will render it in a form that allows it to enter solution. In addition, the enzyme amylase should always be added to ensure that any starch that does dissolve is converted into sugar.

Wheat Wine Wheat is most suited to making a sweet wine of the Madeira style. Much of the character of the wine comes from the use of the brown sugar.

1 lb crushed wheat	450 gms	
1 lb raisins	450 gms	
1 litre grapefruit juice		
2½ lb white sugar	1125 gms	
½ lb demerara sugar	225 gms	
Amylase		
Wine yeast		
Water to one gallon	4.5 litres	

Place the crushed wheat and chopped raisins into the fermenting bucket and cover with two pints of boiling water. Leave for two minutes then add two pints (1.25 litres) of cold water followed by the grapefruit juice. Stir thoroughly and add the sugar, again stirring until all of the white sugar has dissolved. Check that the temperature is within the range 65-70°F (18.5-21°C), then add the yeast and amylase. Cover. Stir every day to ensure that all the sugar has dissolved, any solid that remains will be washed at the straining stage. Because of the nature of the wine which will be slightly oxidised and the high sugar concentration it may be left in the fermentation bucket for fourteen days. Strain and transfer to a demijohn, fit an airlock. Often with this wine a heavy sediment is thrown early in the fermentation. Rack immediately, and top up with half of the demerara sugar dissolved in water. At the second racking check the taste, and if the wine is still sweet top up with water, but if it is dry, or not as sweet as you would wish, make up with the remainder of the brown sugar dissolved in water. This wine benefits from a long maturation period.

Barley and Orange Wine

2 lb crushed barley	900 gms
1 litre orange juice	
1 medium sized orange	
3 lb sugar	1350 gms
Amylase	
Wine yeast	
Water to one gallon	4.5 litres

Place the barley in the bucket and cover with two pints (1.25 litres) of boiling water, leave for two minutes and add two pints of cold water. Then add the orange juice and stir in the sugar until dissolved. Wines made from oranges seldom retain the characteristic flavour of the parent fruit, so to overcome this problem the zest of a fresh fruit should be added. Peel the fruit very thin, no more than $\frac{1}{20}$ inch (1 mm) in depth and add this to the liquid. Ensure that none of the white pith of the peel enters the liquid as this will give the drink a bitter taste. Complete the preparation for fermentation by the addition of the yeast and amylase. Strain after five days, place in a demijohn, top up with water and fit an airlock. Finish in the usual manner.

OTHER WINES

Parsley Wine Parsley gives a very agreeable flavour, reminiscent of elderflowers to a wine and is ideally suited to light white table wines.

4 sprigs parsley	
1 lb sultanas	450 gms
2¾ lb white sugar	1250 gms
1 litre grapefruit juice	
Wine yeast	
Water to one gallon	4.5 litres

Bring the sultanas just to the boil with two pints of water. Pour the liquid and solid into the fermentation vessel, add the sugar and dissolve by stirring. Add two pints (1.25 litres) of cold water and the grapefruit juice. Then add the yeast. Cover and stir daily. Strain the liquid into a demijohn after seven days. Fit an airlock, rack when the wine becomes clear.

Tea Wine Tea is rich in tannin and this gives to a wine a characteristic astringent taste, such wine is often one of the best tawnies that it is possible to brew.

2 pints cold tea	1.25 litres
2 lb bananas	900 gms
1 litre grapefruit juice	
3¼ lb sugar	1460 gms
Wine yeast	
Water to one gallon	4.5 litres

Prepare the tea as for drinking without adding milk or sugar and place in a fermentation bucket. Place the peeled bananas in a saucepan together with two pints (1.25 litres) of water, bring to the boil and simmer for half an hour. Strain the grey liquid into the bucket, add three pounds (1350 gms) of the sugar and dissolve. Add the yeast. Cover and allow to ferment in the bucket until the vigorous working ceases. Transfer to a demijohn, top up with water when there is no danger of the liquid frothing over into the airlock. Rack when there is half an inch (1 cm) of sediment, and top up with sugar syrup made by dissolving the remaining quarter of a pound in sufficient water to fill the container. As with all wines rich in tannin the wine continues to improve for several years.

Birch Sap Wine Birch sap, which can usually only be gathered in sufficient quantities in the third week of March when the liquid is rising up the stem, is one of the most unusual ingredients of winemaking. Unlike all other country wines, due to the lack of acid it is impossible to make a wine the majority of which consists of the main ingredient rather than tap water. You should only attempt to obtain sap from a tree where you know that your equipment will not be disturbed by passers by. Before attempting to extract sap from a birch tree you should always seek the permission of the owner. To obtain birch sap it is necessary to drill a hole, a quarter of an inch in diameter (½ cm) into the trunk of the tree. Select a tree which is about a foot in girth and drill the hole two foot from the base. Fit a piece of plastic tubing into the trunk and allow this to trail into a demijohn or other suitable container. Cover the container, allowing only sufficient room for the tubing to enter. Depending upon the strength of the sap flow it will take from two to seven days to gather sufficient to make one gallon of wine. When the sap has been extracted stop up the hole in the tree, failure to do this will cause the tree to bleed to death.

4 pints birch sap	2.25 litres
1 litre pure grapefruit juice	
2¾ lb sugar	1250 gms
½ lb sultanas	225 gms
Wine yeast	
Water to one gallon	4.5 litres

Chop the sultanas and dissolve the sugar in the minimum quantity of hot water. Place all of the ingredients, except the yeast, into the fermentation bucket and check the temperature, when this lies between 65-70°F (18.5-21°C) add the yeast. Cover the bucket and stir daily. After seven days strain and transfer to a demijohn, fit an airlock. The wine may be drunk when it is clear.

Wallflower Wine Previous generations knew the advantages of making wines from wallflowers. With wallflowers there is virtually no difference in the bouquet of the various different coloured plants. Because the bouquet is so strong, only a small quantity is required.

¼ pint wallflowers	125 ml
½ lb sultanas	225 gms
2½ lbs sugar	1125 gms
2 tsp citric acid	
1 cup of cold tea	
Wine yeast	
Water to 1 gallon	4.5 litres

Strip the petals from the green. Mince the sultanas and place together with the citric acid and cold tea in the fermenting bucket. Add half a gallon of boiling water. Dissolve the sugar in the remaining half gallon of (2.25 litres) water and add to the must. At 70°F (21°C) add the yeast. Cover the bucket, stir daily. After seven days strain, place in the demijohn and fit an airlock.

Index